THE IMPOSTOR

JEAN COCTEAU

THE IMPOSTOR

Translated from the French by
DOROTHY WILLIAMS

LONDON

PETER OWEN

ISBN 0 7206 4370 8

Translated from the French
Thomas L'Imposteur

PETER OWEN LIMITED
73 Kenway Road London SW5 0RE

First British Commonwealth edition 1957
Third impression 1977
© Jean Cocteau 1929
English translation © Peter Owen 1957

Printed in Great Britain by
REDWOOD BURN LIMITED
Trowbridge & Esher

A T THE beginning of the war there was complete
confusion: confusion which persisted until the
end. For, like a fruit, a short war might have
grown and dropped from the tree, whilst a war
prolonged for exceptional reasons, firmly attached
to the branch, went on growing, ever presenting
new problems and new lessons to be learnt.

*   *   *

The Government had just left Paris, or, as one
of its members ingenuously put it, had gone to
Bordeaux to plan the Victory of the Marne.

This victory, which seemed a miracle, has a
simple explanation, as anyone who has been to
school can see. Mischief-makers will always do
better than bookworms, if an unforeseen event
arises to upset the bookworm when he is mechanically repeating his lesson. Yet this protracted confusion, which banished the existing order, was
confusion none the less. The atmosphere fostered
extremes of behaviour.

Paris was quiet. There, the daughter of a distinguished officer of State had converted Dr. Verne's

nursing home into a Red Cross hospital. At least, she had converted the lower part of this magnificent old mansion on the Left Bank, leaving the rest to the civilian patients. She had applied herself to this charitable work with an enthusiasm which nothing but the departure of the Government could extinguish. Then she asked leave to go, explaining to the doctor that she had to follow her father—as if she were not old enough to act for herself.

She went, leaving the wards full of beds and equipment in the hands of the surgeons, the voluntary nurses, and the Sisters of Mercy.

Dr. Verne was a spiritualist. He neglected his many patients because there were first-class specialists attached to the establishment.

Verne, who was suspected of being a heavy drinker, would spent part of the day locked in his study, originally the caretaker's room, which overlooked the courtyard; from this vantage point he hypnotized the staff.

He would order one to limp, another to cough. Nothing amused him more than these absurdities. He had taken in almost everyone in the house with his tricks, and, once under his influence, the

6

patients were at his mercy. They knew him to be eccentric, but they did not realize the extent of his eccentricity. On his daily visits the doctor would consult their temperature charts and make a few well-chosen remarks as he passed from room to room, like a hotel manager moving among his clients.

The Verne house in the rue Jacob had formerly been the hôtel Joyeuse. The building, flanked by new wings, stood between the circular courtyard and the garden. So the trees behind would come as a delightful surprise to the new patient who on his arrival had been dismayed by the gloomy façade.

*   *   *

The princesse de Bormes' daughter slept in one of the rooms, where the panelling was intact, but sprayed with enamel for the sake of hygiene. She had recently had an operation for appendicitis. The princess, who would not leave her, had a small room close by.

Mme de Bormes was one of the few people of

her standing who had to stay in Paris after the Government had left for Bordeaux. Secretly, she was glad of a reason to stay in the capital. She did not believe that Paris would fall. She did not believe it because it was a common belief, and, as is often the case, her scornful incredulity gave her second sight. None the less, people thought her mad. On the very morning of the Government's departure, her friend Pesquel-Duport, who edited the newspaper *Le Jour*, begged her to take her daughter to Bordeaux, and, when she refused, exclaimed that she was staying out of sheer perversity, to hear the band play the *Marche Militaire*.

Her real motives were of a different nature.

She had been a very young widow, for the prince had died in a hunting accident only two years after their marriage. She was Polish. Poland is the land of pianists. Like a virtuoso at the piano, who can invest even the most mediocre compositions with beauty, she fingered the keyboard of life to the maximum effect. Pleasure was a duty to her.

And so this excellent woman would say, "I dislike the poor. I loathe the sick."

It was hardly surprising that such statements should cause a scandal.

She meant to enjoy herself and she knew how to do it. Unlike other women of her position, she had realized that pleasure is not to be found only in particular things, but in one's approach to life in all its aspects. This attitude demands robust good health.

The princess was over forty. She had the face of a little girl, with sparkling eyes which lost their lustre the moment she was bored. And so she hated boredom and loved laughter, which women commonly avoid for fear of wrinkles.

Her health, her way of life, and the originality of her tastes and her behaviour gave her a dreadful reputation.

Now she was purity and magnanimity itself. And this was meaningless to people who see purity and magnanimity as divine ideas which it is sacrilege to use. For, in using these gifts, the princess unbent them and gave them a new brilliance. She wore virtue to suit herself, moulding it to her, as a well-dressed woman wears a coat which hangs too stiffly; and spiritual beauty was so natural to her that it passed unnoticed.

So the hypocritical world judged her, as badly-dressed women judge those who are elegant.

The stars showed that she was born for adventure. Her mother, with child, abandoned, passionately in love, had set herself to find the culprit, who had disappeared some months before. She had found him in a small town in Russia. There, overhearing a conversation behind a door at which she dared not ring, this lovesick woman died of exhaustion and suffering in giving birth to a daughter.

This daughter, Clémence, had spent her early childhood in the company of a drunken servant. When her father died, a cousin took care of her. But this wild, untalkative child, who shielded herself instinctively with her shoulder, grew up suddenly, like the fakirs' rose-bush.

Her cousin was astonished to see that she was restless after going to a ball. She grew, opened out and blossomed, without and within. She was a little minx, and she organized the young people's social events.

At length she met the prince de Bormes, a travelling diplomat, and became engaged to him in four days. The prince was bewitched. She saw her way through him to France and its capital. Paris seemed the only theatre fit to be honoured with her first appearance.

There is always a certain length of time before the first flush of sincerity wears off, and the public, afraid of having betrayed emotion, of having been caught out, forms a set opinion.

At first, the princess took advantage of its surprise at her entrance.

Later, her free and easy manner and her tactlessness offended people.

She brought up subjects which ought to have been left alone, she dwelt on them, and she skated on thin ice in the midst of a stony silence. Everyone hoped she would break her neck.

Once she had entertained, she would aggravate her audience. She entered society as a young sportsman might break into a card-party and upset the game, telling everyone to go and play football. The regular players (young and old) rose from their seats. They soon settled down again, but they resented her.

Yet if this striking, highly-coloured nature offended some, it charmed others. These were the few, the very ones whose verdict, according to Montesquieu, should be accepted in courts of law.

And so, by way of one indiscretion after another,

the princesse de Bormes put her acquaintances through the finest sieve; discarding the mediocre and keeping only the very best.

Seven or eight men, two or three high-minded women became her intimate friends. They were precisely the friends that a designing woman would have wanted, and failed to win.

For the prince's sake the others hid feelings which, after his death, became a secret intrigue against her. The princess saw in this intrigue a means of hitting out and showing her strength, and she made light of the danger. She worked out schemes of her own with her staff-officers.

People deplored her behaviour as unseemly for a woman in mourning. But she had no affection for the prince, and rebelled at playing the heart-broken widow. The prince left her a daughter—Henriette.

Henriette inherited the rapt admiration which had held the prince transfixed in the presence of Mme de Bormes. Clémence was born an actress and her daughter a spectator, and her favourite sight was her mother.

And indeed, she was the loveliest sight in the world, this woman who lived in a wonderland of her own, so that angels seemed to fly round her like birds round a bird-catcher.

If anything worried her, the atmosphere was stifling. A sort of radiance was diffused when she was happy.

This woman, who cared nothing for the first place at social functions, did want the best. The two are not usually the same. At the theatre, she wanted to see and not to be seen. The actors liked her.

At first glance, she saw the war as a theatre. A theatre exclusive to men.

She could not be satisfied with living on the outer edge of this event which was taking place; she felt that she was barred from the only show worth seeing. And for this reason, far from deploring the fact that circumstances kept her in Paris, she blessed them, and thanked her daughter for it.

Paris was not the war. But, alas, it was not far away, and this fearless woman listened to the cannon like those who listen to the orchestra outside a concert-hall, because the doorkeeper will not let them in.

In this thirst for war, the princess was as far from morbidity as possible. Blood, fever, and the deli-

rium of bull-fights did not attract her. She thought
of these things with disgust. She pitied all the
wounded without discrimination. No; she adored
fashions, grave or gay. Danger was in fashion; the
calm was killing her. While young men were burn-
ing up energy and even going so far as to throw
themselves out of windows, she was straining at the
leash. She would have liked events to help and
support her, as the crowd helps a woman to see a
firework display.

Such great gifts are not commonly understood.
They arouse suspicion. The miserly world accuses
the owner of coining money.

In the circumstances, because of the spy scare,
Mme de Bormes was accused of being Polish, in
other words, a spy.

She was well-liked in the rue Jacob. She made
use of this. With her talents she was soon on the
track of an ingenious way of taking part in events.

The lower part of the house was a first-aid
centre, but it was empty. She thought of filling it.
This involved making up a convoy, recruiting cars
and drivers, obtaining the necessary passes, and
bringing back from the front as many casualties
as possible. She dangled the Military Cross in front

of the doctor, who collaborated with her. He called for action stations in his hospital, which was for all the world like the Sleeping Beauty's castle, shook off his chloroformic stupor, heaped praise on the radiographer's wife for her patriotism. Bit by bit, Clémence assembled a great machine.

The most difficult task was to find cars and drivers. The princess could not get over it. She thought there were a lot of people wanting to lead a double life and look death in the face.

Eventually she collected eleven cars, including her own limousine and the hospital ambulance.

In a flash she had seen the advantages of the dispute which was now at its height.

This was the period when the old uniform, in the process of changing to the new, had become unrecognizable. Everyone wore it in his own way. And this cast-off kit, so comical in town, was magnificent in the armies—rank upon rank of ragamuffins.

The princess inferred the amazing success of this revolution from the roads strewn with champagne bottles, chairs, and pianolas.

She hardly thought, I must confess, of the masquerading, the false teeth, the pot-bellies and

death's nauseating smells, of the way that hunters
and game alike would soon become plants, Siamese
twins linked by a thread of mud and despair.

She could scent heroism as a horse scents the
stable. She sped hotfoot after our troops. She
flaunted her white cap. She went in and out of her
daughter's room twenty times a day to tell her of
the progress she was making.

*   *   *

The main courtyard that had been so imposing
was no longer recognizable with its paving-stones
choked with grass. Engines roared, cars backed into
each other, drivers yelled. The princess, dragging
Verne after her, was allotting duties.

Yet, like Colonel Renard's earth-bound airship
which, when its inventor gave the famous order to
let go, as he sat in it by the fireside with his wife
at her knitting, rose four inches, and then fell flat,
the convoy did not leave on the appointed day. It
needed a red pass.

Madame de Bormes thought she had persuaded
the authorities to give her the Open Sesame of

the war in one visit to the Invalides. All she had
obtained was a police-pass which would take them
no farther than Juvisy.

The disappointment was all the greater because
the party had set out at dawn amidst the cheers of
the dairywomen and the staff. They had to retrace
their steps and straggle back dejectedly three hours
later.

But the impetus had been given. Nothing could
stop it. The princess began her appeals all over
again, and from this day forward the courtyard
looked like a factory.

*   *   *

Strange mushrooms sprouted from the cracks in
this courtyard.

The war, like a thunderstorm, had its own flora
and fauna.

Mme Valiche was an example of it.

Stage-struck, but not for the same reasons as the
princess, she had introduced herself to the convoy
as nurse-in-chief. She brought with her a bad
dentist, Dr. Gentil, and passed him off as a hospital

surgeon. She was as ugly, common and grasping as
Madame de Bormes was beautiful, distinguished
and selfless. The two women had in common a flair
for intrigue. But one schemed for her amusement,
the other for her profit.

In the troubled waters of this chaotic war, Mme
Valiche saw a splendid opportunity to fish for a
miraculous draught of compensations. She loved
Dr. Gentil, and she spurred him on. In addition
to this motive she derived a morbid pleasure from
horrors.

The princess confused this enthusiasm with her
own. She was soon to see how very different they
were.

Madame Valiche was the widow of a colonel who
had died of the fever at Tonking. She would
describe his death and the hazardous journey of
the coffin which she was bringing back to France.
Ultimately this coffin, insecurely attached to the
crane which was hoisting it on board ship, had
fallen into the water. She consoled herself with the
dentist. He had a black beard, a yellow face, and
eyes like a houri.

The pair were never without police jackets and
caps. Madame Valiche had sewn stripes on to her

lover's jacket and her own. She would follow
Clémence into the offices, where her poise and her
armlet worked wonders.

But even with so much charm on one hand and
so much cunning on the other, the convoy was still
an idea, with members who pestered the wounded
and behaved more like ministers than nurses.

*   *   *

As he walked down the street one evening, a
young soldier saw this noisy, congested courtyard
through the open gates. He stopped, leant against
one of the gate-posts, and watched the commotion
with the air of Napoleon watching the Clubs.

He hesitated a long time, then entered and went
over to the mechanics.

He looked so young to be in uniform that he
might have been a soldier's child. But his youth
was doubtful in the light of the narrow lance-
corporal's stripe on the sleeve of his small blue
tunic. His good looks, his fresh open face, introduced him in less time than any certificate.

In ten minutes he was helping everyone and he

knew everything. He even knew that General d'Ancourt had been brought in the night before, and had one of the ground-floor rooms to himself. The General was a friend of the chief surgeon in the rue Jacob, and the surgeon had managed to have him transferred from the Buffon Hospital. His leg had to be amputated. He was delirious. His friend had almost given up hope.

As he moved from group to group, the young soldier eventually came across Dr. Verne who, with the princess, was drawing up a list of the members of the society.

"Who are you?" asked Verne with his usual bluntness.

"Guillaume Thomas de Fontenoy," was the reply.

"Relative of General de Fontenoy?"

The General was appearing in all the headlines at this time.

"Yes, his nephew."

The reply took effect at once, for the doctor always had his Cross in mind. It was his guiding star.

"Good Lord!" he exclaimed. "Are you one of us?"

"I am General d'Ancourt's secretary," said the

young man. "But unhappily he has no need of my services, and I pass the time as best I can without going too far away from him."

"But you are a gift of the gods!" cried the princess. "If the General is saved, he will still have to stay in his room for months. I enrole you. I am your General."

While Verne felt his Cross growing larger and larger, Clémence visualized the countless uses of the magic name. This woman, who could not see a trap a yard in front of her, could see into the future. Once again, she was right.

*   *   *

Although he had the same name as the proverbial doubter, Guillaume Thomas was an impostor. He was not General de Fontenoy's nephew, nor was he in any way related to him. He was born in Fontenoy near Auxerre where, historians suppose, Charles the Bald won the victory of Fontanet in 841.

When war was declared, he was sixteen. He was furious. He cursed his age. He had a thirst for adventure from his grandfather, a sea-captain. He was an orphan and he lived in Montmartre with his aunt, a pious old maid who let him run wild because she was only interested in saving his soul, regardless of other people's.

Guillaume had already found falsehood to be a prelude to adventure; he made himself older than he was, told the neighbours that he was going to join up, that he would have a special permit, and one fine day he appeared in a uniform which he had borrowed from a friend. In this disguise he roamed the streets and hung about the barracks and the gates of the Invalides.

"I am on the small-arms course," he told his aunt. Things were so gloomy and so unsettled that anything seemed possible.

Like children when they are playing, he gradually came to believe in the game. He gave himself a stripe.

No-one challenged him. He had no fears. He was proud that civilians should give him a second look as he passed by. One day, when he showed an auxiliary cyclist a family document with the word Fontenoy on it, the cyclist thought his name was Thomas de Fontenoy, and asked him the same question as Verne. For the first time, Guillaume replied in the affirmative, and from that day the title became part of his equipment.

*　　　*　　　*

You see what kind of an impostor Guillaume was. His sort are a race apart. They live half-way between reality and make-believe. They are distinguished, not lowered, by the deception which they practise. Guillaume took people in without malice. The story will show that he took himself in. Like any child, cabby or horse, he forgot what he really was.

He would have been very surprised if anyone had pointed out that he was in danger of being sent to prison.

To explain his strange immunity I will give an example of the sort of scene which took place again and again.

Guillaume was in the place des Invalides with Madame Valiche. He was mad on firearms. He wore a regulation revolver on his belt. He sported a forage cap and Dr. Verne's Red Cross armlet, trimmed with gold braid.

A captain stopped him. The conversation went like this: —

"You there!"

"Yes Sir?"

"What sort of uniform is this? Why are you wearing a revolver and a Red Cross armlet?"

"But Sir . . ."

"And what about that cap? What sort of cap is that?"

"Its the Cyr cap, Sir."

"What's that? Are you at Saint-Cyr? Don't make a fool of me. What's your name?"

"Thomas de Fontenoy, Sir."

"De Fontenoy? Are you a relative of the General?"

"His nephew, Sir."

"They say he has driven back the German left wing."

"That's so Sir."

"Now listen—between ourselves, I know that uniforms are being worn in the most unorthodox ways, but don't wear an armlet *and* a revolver. Take your pick. Wear one or the other. Because you have come across me this time," added the

soldier paternally, "but you may come across a
fool."

*   *   *

As a matter of routine the princess put Guillaume into the picture. She would not leave this
talisman. In forty-eight hours she had obtained
what she had been trying to find for four weeks.
There was no time wasted at the name of Fontenoy.
Guillaume was scolded, patted, had his ears
tweaked, and came away with the permits.

An orderly who knew the passwords was even
found to travel with the convoy on the front seat
of the leading car. This car was for Madame
Valiche and the doctor, the second for the princess,
and the others followed in any order. Their drivers
were a shirt-maker, a writer, and a man who was
out of work.

They left at 11 o'clock at night.

The irregularity of such an arrangement was
made even worse when Madame de Bormes'
mechanic received his marching orders and she
put in his place a poor Russian painter who hardly

spoke our language at all, and had become a driver for love. The princess helped him to live. He worshipped her. He was a bad driver. But he did not have to drive fast, and he followed the leading car.

Madame Valiche and Dr. Gentil, who had never had a car, enjoyed the drive and felt they were in for a bit of luck.

They put their feet up on the crates of dry biscuits, oranges, and Cordial-Médoc which Madame de Bormes had brought for the wounded. They stretched themselves out, patted their stripes, and kissed each other when the car crossed a gutter. The car stopped at every post.

"Who goes there? Who goes there?" A forbidding shadow blocked the way. The orderly, a clockwork toy, jumped out of his seat, spoke into the shadow's ear and climbed back in again, and the convoy went on, crawling up slopes, passing through villages in ruins.

There was a ridiculous interlude when Madame de Bormes, who had Guillaume in her car, looked through the back window and saw the hospital ambulance lit up like a shop-window in the rue de la Paix. Dr. Verne was in his seat, and the radiographer's wife, who was suspected of being Verne's mistress, sat alone in this lighting, bolt upright on a pile of pillows.

She was playing at being an angel. Smiling, her eyes half-shut, one hand on the switch, she appeared and disappeared at her will as they drove through the countryside.

Madame de Bormes asked Guillaume to lean out of the door and tell the doctor to put the light off. It was dangerous to play at angels in these parts, where a glimmer of lamplight might have you shot for a spy.

Clémence and Guillaume were kindred spirits. Like children yearning after a cake, they had their noses glued to the window-pane.

They were going behind the scenes of the drama. Now they were close to the stage, and they could gaze on the solitude, the trees to left and right, the night resounding with gun-fire.

They were like music-worshippers in the gallery listening to Stravinsky, leaning over the dark pit.

The endless drive did not tire them. They bore with the brown smell of the charnel-house, the monotonous noise of the sky-line crumbling.

In a short time this noise would no longer be as

distant as the slam of a side-door heard from the
fifth floor. It would shake the car and surround it
with lights. Secretly the princess and Guillaume
each looked forward to that great moment.

*　　　*　　　*

What mysterious law brings together a Guillaume,
a Madame Valiche, and a princesse de Bormes like
quicksilver? Their spirit of adventure draws them
together from the ends of the earth.

*　　　*　　　*

Suddenly the leading car turned into a side-street
and stopped dead. They could make out railings
and pillars. What was going on? A simple matter.
Verne had property near Paris. He wanted to take
a hundred pots of geraniums there. Fearing sarcas-
tic remarks from the princess, he had not breathed
a word of it to her, but had furtively filled the
cars with pots and agreed with Madame Valiche
that they should make this tremendous detour.

And so instead of getting nearer the lines, they were going away from them.

When the princesse de Bormes learnt of the scheme, she was furious. The doctor was unloading his geraniums. She grabbed him by the sleeve. But just as she was going to burst into a torrent of reproaches, he turned to her with such a comical face that she burst out laughing. For he was wearing glasses with a rubber shield, which gave him a Greek profile. Her laughter saved him. The princess could not control it. She went back into the car, laughing till she cried. This irrepressible laughter went on all the time the doctor and his collaborators were moving the pots. It was subsiding when an embarrassed Verne came to apologize to her. She began to laugh more than ever.

"Here is a woman I could get on with," thought Guillaume. She was his sort. He was sorry for his pious aunt. "Do you believe in God, madam?" he asked. "Yes," replied Clémence, "particularly when I am afraid. Why, in railway trains, for instance."

*　　　　*　　　　*

They reached M. at dawn.

The steep street was crowded. The Bishop, conspicuous in his cape, was already busy there. He would leave this street for nothing but his throne. He was ambitious; he enjoyed ceremony and honours. And he was not prepared to lose a scrap of his reputation.

He stood dramatically, his robe held high, showing his mauve ankles, as if the departed German flood had left puddles behind it.

He had galvanized the town, silenced the Mayor, and, captain of his vessel, he reigned supreme.

The women kissed his amethyst, the men hung on his commands. Handsome and puffed up, he was a fabulous fuchsia.

At the sight of the convoy crossing his town, he frowned, and committed to memory the appearance of the cars. The princess would have liked to receive his blessing, but Gentil was a free-thinker. He did not even believe in spiritualism, as did Madame Valiche, who was amazed at this total incredulity.

"The monster, he doesn't believe in anything," she said.

"Oh yes," replied the dentist witheringly, "I do believe. I believe in vibrations in the ether."

They thought the Bishop ridiculous.

"He's in evening dress from sunrise," exclaimed Madame Valiche.

"Good day to you, Dominus vobiscum amen," mumbled the doctor, and their car passed on, the others behind it, under the hostile glare of the great man.

Towns can be burned down; Bishops cannot. They paid for this mistake the following morning. At the time, the most disturbed among them was a young ordinand. He was looking for his brother, of whom he had had no news, and had been allowed to follow the convoy. He was curled up on the seat of the last car; but, as they passed, the eagle eye of the Bishop had counted every button of his cassock. He felt that he was lost. Thinking of him, Madame Valiche said to the doctor, "poor vobiscum, he must be at his wits' end." She always called priests 'vobiscum.' But the doctor was asleep. Madame Valiche wrapped a shawl around him and took his lifeless hand.

The sky was pink. Cocks were crowing. Cannon shook the window-panes. Lawns, smoke, limbers, horses, were pink. Beside a field of pink beetroot, shameless dragoons were squatting down, pink moons upturned. Others in their shirt-sleeves were washing their faces. The sight of these women struck them dumb. The princess, waving her hand, stared at their pink faces, round eyes and open mouths until they were out of sight.

"We are in the wings," she said to herself, "and these are the actors, the walkers-on, dressing for their parts."

They passed apple-tree after apple-tree, post after post, until they came to a straggling market-town where the casualties were being taken into a round tent pitched on the square like a circus. Madame Valiche's car stopped. She was not looking for the fire, she was looking for its victims.

The young doctors were pleased but surprised to receive this unexpected support. Someone opened a crate and handed bottles round, and the surgeon-major was informed. The surgeon-major did not look kindly on these civilians. He refused to give the princesse de Bormes the casualties she asked for.

"No, madame!" he exclaimed. "Straw is luxury to wounded men. They need nothing else. In any case, *can't the wounded be left alone?* There will be a *glut* of wounded in this war."

All the members of the convoy listened without breathing a word. The princess was ready to burst. But it takes vulgarity to crush vulgarity. The major was insensitive to anything else. He loathed Clémence's charm. Madame Valiche won him over. She threw in Guillaume's name with remarkable success. The major was transformed. His assistants unbent. The major would not hand over his casualties, but he would allow them to give the men small comforts and dress their wounds. He showed them the way to a farm nine kilometres away where the casualties were in such bad condition that those in charge would certainly give them up

Inside the tent about thirty martyred men lay in agony on bundles of straw. A nauseating smell prevailed, nameless, rank and sickly, tinged with the dark musk of gangrene. The faces of some were swollen, yellow, covered with flies; others had the colouring, the leanness and the gestures of El Greco's monks. They all looked as if they had just been in a fire-damp explosion. Blood was caked on their ragged uniforms, and as the uniforms had lost their precise colour and shape, it was not clear which were German soldiers and which ours. A heavy stupor made them one.

33

Madame de Bormes was afraid that going into such a place might make her feel sick. She made a superhuman effort to pull herself together. For she was great-grand-daughter of a man who had smashed a glass and swallowed it rather than give himself up.

Madame Valiche was a real surprise. At last she was in her element. This Morgue transformed her. She joked and used barrack-room language as she slit greatcoats, prepared bandages, rolled them up, brought out syringes, gave injections, and refused or gave water to the men.

"Hey, my girl!" she called to the princess, who was as awkward as Madame Valiche might have been at a ball. "Hey, get to work! Pass me the scissors. No, no, don't unbutton that. Cut it! Cut it! The princess is paying. Not you, princess; the other."

She laughed, kneeling by the wreck of a man.

Madame de Bormes' revulsion almost drove her to regret her undertaking. But she saw that what Madame Valiche said carried weight, that the young officers treated her as a colleague, and that she, the princess, was the one who was making a bad impression.

She looked for Guillaume. Guillaume lost no sleep over Christian charity. Armed with his name, he was inspecting the armoury and requisitioning revolvers.

*   *   *

In the evening they left for the farm. It was raining and it was cold. The farm was in the open country. A mound in the middle of the farmyard made the muddy water run into the stables. In the stables was a German first-aid party that had been captured. There were only enemy wounded.

They held council in the rain, by the light of a swaying lantern held by the drowsy surgeon-major. He asked nothing better than to see the back of these vermin, he said.

The German major held a pitchfork and a lantern. This was his system of classification. The men who had most life in them shouted the loudest. He handed over their field record cards to the dentist. Then they brought the poor creatures out of the mire and carried them into the yard.

A light fell on the face of one of them who was

lying on a stretcher. He was young. He was alive; both his hands had been blown off. With his tongue he kept on catching up a little chain that he wore round his neck, and taking the medals in his mouth. He was asking for a miracle, no doubt: to wake up in his bed in Germany, with his hands. The major took the medals out of his mouth by hooking up the chain on one of the prongs of his fork. The cripple let him, and then began again.

When they put the poor man on his feet, he had a dreadful reflex. He put out his stumps to take hold of the copper rail on the ambulance. He fainted, and the nurses lifted him in.

"Phew!" said our major to the Prussian major, "are you satisfied?" Arr you setizfied? he pronounced it, to help him understand. But the prisoner bit his lip and gave his instructions in signs.

"That's annoying," said Madame Valiche, pushing wisps of hair back under her cap with filthy hands, "bags for the Val-de-Grâce. Nix for the rue Jacob. The event's postponed."

The princess almost admired this woman.

"But, madame," she asked her with the artlessness which made society people think she was

casting aspersions, "what do you do when there is
no war on?"

"What do I do? I go riding in the Bois de
Boulogne every morning. White harness, rosettes
on the bridle. The Ritz from five to seven. I recite.
I take lessons from Romuald. I recite on Saturdays
at the Petit Palais for the *Club des aviateurs
honoraires*. Don't think that I always wear a jacket.
I have tastes of my own. I like seductive dresses,
anklets, bouquets of rather faded violets and hats
with Rembrandtesque feathers. Do you know *La
Fiancée du Timbalier?*"

Madame de Bormes felt like a diver going down
to the sea-bed. Madame Valiche was ushering her
into a maze.

"Olé! Olé!" were her parting words. "I am
going back to the Boches." She swung round in a
pirouette and danced a snatch of a Spanish step.

"I got to know Gentil at the Tooth-Picks Ball,
you know," she said with a Belgian accent, at the
stable-door. "He was dressed as a Boer, and I went
as Carmen. A black eye is watching you."

She disappeared.

The princesse de Bormes could not imagine
Madame Valiche in any way other than on the

roads at night with her hands in the pockets of her man's tunic, or, in the daytime, emptying chamber-pots. She thought she was well-travelled and knew what the mass of people was like, but she did not realize that, like the earth, she was always surrounded by her own atmosphere, and, like the earth, she could hardly believe in life on other worlds.

This character, faced with so much horror, was bound to undergo an ordeal. For, however spirited, original and self-assured a woman of the world— although condemned by the world—may be, she has developed nevertheless on the amateur stage, and the first contact with a real theatre paralyses the freedom of her movements.

The princess was soon to recover. She was not one to suffer a failure. She could not stand in the middle of this farm like a reproach. She must laugh at Madame Valiche, and get to work. In a moment her decision was made. She braced herself to it. And when Madame Valiche came out of the stable shouting, "I've a fine cripple·with no legs!" the princess replied in a clear voice, "Would you like me to help you carry him?"

On the return journey in the car, Guillaume

emptied his pockets, full of German cartridge-cases and epaulets. He showed this sinister collection to Madame de Bormes.

Disillusioned at first, like an actress at her first appearance, by the foul smell in the wings, she was gradually getting used to it.

She was sleepy. Guillaume was not. He made her comfortable with cushions, and went to sleep before she did.

His head was lolling and his tongue showed between his half-open lips. His hand, which rested on the door-handle, slipped off it with a thud. He looked like the wounded.

Madame de Bormes fell asleep too.

*　　　　*　　　　*

"Ten minutes halt, refreshments! All change!"

Madame Valiche opened the door.

"Where are we?" asked Clémence, who was still half in a dream.

Guillaume jumped out of his dream on to the road.

"We are at M., fair princess, and the casualties

39

are shouting that they're glad of it."

Indeed, a strange moaning sound came through the cold night, curses and banging on the partitions.

"They are in pain," said Clémence. "The road is full of pot-holes."

"That didn't stop you sleeping. And its for their own good. We're taking them to bye-byes. They don't know their luck. But that's not the snag. We're stuck. Five cars without petrol!"

It was so. There was not a moment to lose. The princess and Madame Valiche would have to take their cars to find petrol. On enquiry, they found that the Bishop alone could give permission for petrol to be requisitioned. It was six o'clock in the morning. The moans of the wounded forced Madame de Bormes to a decision. They thought it would be good policy to take along the ordinand, who had not found a trace of his brother. They bundled him into the car where Gentil was dozing, and lined up in front of the Bishop's lawn. The princess rang the bell. An old maid came to the door. A young priest followed her. Madame de Bormes explained their predicament to him. The young priest, who was doing up his cassock, was sorry for them, and asked the maid to bring out some bread and jam, while he informed his Lordship.

His Lordship, ever at the breach, had been peering through his shutters and had recognized the remnants of the procession. He dressed, came downstairs at top speed, and, refusing to hear a word, he thundered at Clémence. He was pale with anger. His reproof was on the subject of their crossing the town the day before. He *alone* commanded the convoys. He had *absolute* control over the Health Service, papers meant no more to him than his first pair of breeches, and he wouldn't give them a drop of petrol.

"Oh! you're riding roughshod over me!" exclaimed the Bishop—a good man, but blinded by Richelieu, and who, in any case, *saw red*. "Well, so be it. Sort yourselves out."

"Come along," he snapped to the young priest. Then, leaving the princess behind, he crossed the hall and opened the outer door.

Alas, an apotheosis awaited him.

On the return journey Madame Valiche and Gentil had emptied the crates. Around them was all the filth and the chaos of a dining-car. They were drunk on Cordial-Médoc. Their affection was undisguised. From his lawn the Bishop caught sight of the abandoned couple, the bottles, the ordinand. He shuddered. Madame Valiche opened one crazy eye.

"Quickly, my love, quickly," she called to the doctor, "give me your lips, for the priests are here!"

When she came out, Madame de Bormes could only see the Bishop's back. He was retreating towards the cathedral in a shower of fine rain, gathering up his robe for all he was worth, as he had done the day before.

*   *   *

Neither Madame Valiche nor Gentil were in a fit state to realize the infamy of their conduct.

Madame Valiche hung round her lover's neck singing Manon. The ordinand was in tears. In this watery sight there was something beyond repair.

Guillaume saved the day. He had been to see the Mayor, and let drop the name of Fontenoy. The Mayor, delighted that his authority should be recognized and the Bishop overlooked, gave can after can.

The orgiastic couple were removed. They were asleep. The tanks were filled, and the plaintive procession moved on again.

* * *

After that Madame de Bormes often suffered pangs of conscience on the dark roads, as she listened to the moans of the wounded. She wondered whether she was not dealing the death-blow to dying men by trying to do her utmost for them. The roads between the lines and the capital, which were growing longer and longer, were broken up by the heavy vehicles. Every bump was purgatory to these men. Was it not better to leave them on the spot, in spite of the lack of attention? They would die in peace.

But when the rue Jacob centre was full, and she visited them at the Buffon Hospital, the Peupliers, or the Val-de-Grâce, she realized that this pleasure of hers was not criminal.

Quite on her own, this admirable woman was

giving the civilian and military leaders a forecast
of an organization which would not be formed
until much later.

*   *   *

When her daughter was well again, Madame de
Bormes returned to her home in the avenue Montaigne. She went backwards and forwards between
the avenue and the hospital, sometimes even going
direct from her home to join the convoy at the
gates of Paris.

Guillaume was the spoilt child of the house. He
had a room there, which saved him from going
back to his aunt's house in Montmartre after
particularly exhausting trips. In any case, his aunt
was far from his thoughts. Guillaume went in to
see her for ten minutes in the week, excusing himself on the grounds that he had an affair on—a job
as liaison officer.

"I have an affair, my affair," he would say, as
gay dogs used to do. He filled his room with helmet
spikes and fragments of shells.

44

Their baptism of fire awaited Clémence de Bormes and Guillaume at Rheims. As they approached from the hills, they saw the martyred town lying below them. A dark pall of smoke hung over it, stretching far beyond, like the smoke of a ship at sea.

Grass grew in the town, trees sprouted from windows. Houses gaped open, showing the flowered wallpaper of their bedrooms. In one there was still a chest of drawers and a picture-frame on the wall. From the edge of another hung a bed.

The cathedral was a mountain of old lace.

The military doctors, unable to carry out their duties because of the heavy bombardment, awaited a lull in the cellars of the *Golden Lion*. There were three hundred casualties at the convent and the hospital. No-one could be evacuated and no-one could be fed, because, in wartime, Rheims was under the protection of a town who would offer her no assistance. The wounded died of their wounds, of hunger, thirst, tetanus and the enemy fire. At the hospital, a gunner had just been told that the only hope of saving him was to amputate his leg without chloroform; pallid, he was smoking a last cigarette before the ordeal when a shell

smashed the surgical instruments, and killed two
medical officers outright.

No-one dared to face the gunner again. Gangrene
must have crept over him like ivy over a statue.

Such scenes took place a dozen times a day. For
a hundred and fifty wounded the Sisters of Mercy
had one glass of sour milk and half a pork sausage.
In a long shell-riddled room, a priest administered
the sacrament from man to man, forcing the teeth
apart with the blade of a knife.

The convoy could offer little assistance, but the
officers gave Gentil messages asking for help. They
lived with the noise of their own ear-splitting shells
whistling above them, and the German shells, that
set a black seal of thunder and death on their
smooth despatches.

In the town, confusion had reached its height,
nerves were at breaking point. Spies seemed to be
everywhere, and spies were soon shot. The princess,
Madame Valiche and Guilluame found a patrol
actually threatening the Russian painter with his
life. He had been found sketching the cathedral.
The name of Fontenoy saved him, and prevented
the other members of the party from having to
share his experience.

This unbearable atmosphere stimulated Clémence and Guillaume. They were second only to Madame Valiche, who amazed everyone at the two dressing stations with her boundless enthusiasm.

She suggested that they should fill the cars with casualties, leave her at Rheims with the doctor, and return the following day for another load. The princess and Guillaume wanted to stay behind too.

"When my car is empty, it holds two men," said Clémence. "We can't possibly take their place."

Wrapped in blankets, they slept in the cellars of the *Golden Lion*. Shells rocked the town as storm-waves rock a ship. It was shaken to the very core.

The enemy guns were aiming at the gasometer. They circled it, they groped hesitantly, like a blind man groping for a door-knob. This threat finally set their nerves on edge.

Guillaume admired the courage of Clémence de Bormes; she admired his. It was soon clear that Guillaume's courage was a product of immaturity and the princess's of inexperience. The princess had seen the very worst. She had seen a horse trampling in its own entrails as it turned a street-corner, a group of gunners blown to pieces at their stations. Yet she thought herself to be invulnerable. Being almost the only woman in the town, she fancied that death had a well-bred respect for her sex, and she courted it fearlessly. But when she was on her way from the convent to the hospital, and saw a poor townswoman and her child struck down in an explosion only fifty yards away, she suddenly realized that shells do not spare women, and was smitten with such fear as only complex natures can feel. She began to scream, and ran round in circles calling for Guillaume.

When he arrived, Guillaume was limping. He had been blown over while he was ferreting in the rubble, and had come out unhurt but for a blow on the knee from a falling beam. He was green.

Clémence wrung her hands. She called herself an unworthy mother, and begged Guillaume to bring her daughter to the spot at once.

This was easier said than done. The cars were not due to return until the evening.

The rest of the day was purgatory. Madame Valiche took care of Clémence, who was trembling in every limb.

All the cars came back except one—the one which was driven by the Parasite. This was their nickname for the man who was out of work. The Germans had aimed at the convoy, a suspicious anthill on the hill-slope, trying to pick off cars like pawns. One of them had succeeded in making queen at the expense of the Parasite's pawn, and not a trace of him remained.

They were to wait for nightfall to cover their departure.

The princess refused to wait. While the Russian painter was turning the starting-handle, a heavy shell, directed at the gasometer, fell on the house in front of their car. They were covered with plaster and their windows were blown out.

In this car, uncomfortable but covered with glory, Clémence and Guillaume left Rheims, oblivious of the Russian's reckless steering.

And then Guillaume heard that incorrigible woman murmur, "Come on, let us go back. How absurd to have been afraid!"

*   *   *

There are some men who have everything and cannot convince one of it, rich men so poor and

noblemen so common that the incredulity with
which they meet makes them shy and gives them
an unconvincing manner. The most beautiful
pearls are artificial on some women. On the other
hand, artificial pearls look real on others. In the
same way there are some men who inspire blind
confidence and enjoy privileges which they cannot
claim by right. Guillaume Thomas was of this
happy breed.

He was believed. He did not have to take precautions nor count the cost. A star of falsehood
led him straight to his goal. And so he never had
the preoccupied, hunted look of the trickster.
Without knowing how to swim or how to skate he
could say 'I skate and I swim.' Everyone had seen
him on the ice and in the water.

A special fairy casts this spell at birth. Some men
who had gifts from no other fairy are successful.

Guillaume never did reflect on his behaviour or
think "How will I get out of this?" "I'm cheating,"
"I'm a wretch," or "I'm a clever man." He went
on, wrapt in his fairy-tale.

The more he lived his part, the more absorbed
in it he became, playing it with convincing verve
and frankness.

For some time he had had a new toy: to describe the death of his cousins before their father's very eyes. His ridiculous story was crudely drawn and coloured, like a chap-book illustration.

His synthesis, like these illustrations, was striking, and seemed more life-like than life itself. It appealed to that element of childishness in his listeners which is present in every one of us. Occasionally he touched up the picture with a bit of gold. He was taken in himself. Tears came to his eyes. No-one could listen to him without being moved.

As he never had to be on his guard—which causes the rogue's downfall—he would relate this heroic·episode in the princess's home, at table, in the presence of expert soldiers. He took in civilians and soldiers alike, proving that the truth, even when it is false, comes out of the mouths of babes.

*   *   *

People were returning to Paris. Those who had taken to their heels and deserted her were straggling back one by one. They all found an apology for their departure to offer to the people who had not left, and these were few and far between. Some used their service as an excuse, others their little girl, their old mother or their own important person that might have been taken as a hostage by the Germans, Others pleaded their duty to the nation.

Pesquel-Duport, who edited *Le Jour,* known to his intimate friends as *The Editor,* one of the ten in Madame de Bormes' set, tried to persuade her that she had been wrong, although circumstances had proved her right; that, for once, fate had been as wild and as lovable as she, and that it was all very well to say that Klück had not entered Paris, he had entered the city in principle if not in fact.

In principle. Clémence was extra-lucid just because she had no principles, and similarly, because our success was contrived without principles, it defied common sense.

*   *   *

Close friends who are used to meeting in the same place usually hate to find a newcomer there.

But Guillaume was an exception to the rule.

"I saw your father quite often in the House," Pesquel-Duport told him.

Spoilt child he was, spoilt child he remained. Spoilt by more people.

He had told Clémence that he had a pain in the knee caused by a splinter from the shell which had smashed General d'Ancourt's thigh. This explosion became an exploit. His heroism put him among the men, and his chap-book illustration opened every heart to him.

For, as a matter of self-respect and not through cunning, he had never betrayed his surprise on his first journeys to the lines.

Besides, Rheims was one of the princess's stories. He left it to her. The truth made him feel all the uneasiness associated with falsehood. Rheims did not interest him, it made him unhappy.

*   *   *

Guillaume's best public was Madame de Bormes' daughter Henriette. For we have said that she was born a spectator. Until then only one great actor, her mother, had held the stage. Now she was watching two.

Henriette, brought up without the faintest superstition of caste, title or wealth, had always seen her mother judge men for what they were worth, and rank artists as high as sovereigns. But she was very young, rarely went out, and seldom had the opportunity of meeting unusual men.

Thanks to the war, so conducive to chance meetings on the railways, she was not only seeing such a man, but he was her own age and they were living close to each other.

No need to say what effect the tales which brought tears to the eyes of veteran soldiers would have on this innocent soul.

She was very fond of Guillaume. In her thoughts she confused him with her mother and, as her mother treated him as a son, she saw nothing wrong in the confusion.

The princess, as we have said, blasted her way through walls; she did not read the writing on them. She never even noticed this rose opening—a wonderful contrivance. Nor did Guillaume. But youth has its infectious diseases. Artificial as he was, Guillaume was without artifice. His pure heart had a far deeper understanding of things than his childish mind.

Guillaume was learning about life greedily since he had set foot in the hospital courtyard. He had begun to live in that courtyard. Without dreaming of congratulating himself on his good luck, he was growing richer, developing, profiting more every day.

Everyone has a monkey on his left shoulder and a parrot on his right. Without any effort on Guillaume's part, his parrot repeated the talk of the privileged classes, his monkey aped its gestures. And so he ran no risk, unlike eccentrics who are adopted by society one week and discarded the next. He dug himself in and seemed to have been born and bred there.

His name confirmed it.

Only one intimate friend frowned on Guillaume. The Editor.

He had been madly in love with the princesse de Bormes for five years. The genius of this journalist was nothing but great patience. He wanted *Le Jour*: he got it. He wanted to be rich: he was. He wanted to marry this widow who was still young, whose brilliant gifts, eclipsed by the worldly environment, would help his work and shine in the intellectual world.

Pesquel-Duport had faith in the intellectual world. He belonged to the period of the salons. He would have liked a salon. He did not realize that only the players and the puppets of art are named on the official prize list, and that her authors stay in the shade. In his dreams Clémence sat opposite him at a table laden with flowers and crystal, surrounded by the most elegant women and the most famous men.

When he pleaded with her, the princess would reply:

"My dear Editor, do wait. We must wait. It would not be true to say that I was in love with you. With you or anyone else, for that matter. But certainly, of all the men I know, you are the one whom I dislike least."

She was sincere. She did not find his face ugly. Pesquel-Duport was fifty-three and his hair was snow-white.

He thought himself more than a match for anyone. So he was in trials of strength, but he lacked deep insight, the insight which is so rare in high places because it allows of no choice.

56

A really profound man does not climb, he tries
the depths. Long after his death his column is
found buried; all at once, or gradually, in pieces.
While the big mediocre intellects, composed of
good judgment and irony, climb to the first cornice
of power unhampered.

The lack of insight in this ambitious man
appealed to Clémence. For if she was not a profound person, at least, like some insects, she had a
probe with which, in spite of her lack of method,
she penetrated to the heart of things.

So this crazy woman passed the judgments of
Tiresias.

Pesquel-Duport saw this faculty without understanding it, and was quite happy to follow her
advice. But he was right about one thing which
his good judgment helped him to grasp; that highly
intelligent women often have a masculine intellect
which upsets their balance and disturbs them,
while the princess was a true woman, and owed
her abilities to her own sex alone.

In his eyes she was Eve, naked and primitive,
eating the apple she wanted and contentedly
leaving Paradise, a well-ordered house.

Pesquel-Duport knew that the princess's conduct

was beyond reproach. This certainty did not prevent him from being jealous.

The affairs of Cherubino and the Countess, Jean-Jacques and Madame de Warens, Fabrice and la Sansévérina blighted his view of the relationship between Clémence and Guillaume. He thought that Guillaume was in love with his protectress and that she enjoyed his attentions.

There his good judgment failed him. Guillaume, roused by Madame de Bormes, brought out of childhood by her, gave the fruits of it to Henriette. He was rather overwhelmed by the princess. He found her in Henriette, but at his own level.

Occasionally this accomplished actor would go down into the dark auditorium to sit by Henriette and applaud her mother. So Henriette was like wives who, after a show, receive the loving attentions which the star dancer arouses in their husbands.

Guillaume clothed this little girl in the princess's attractions, and, as she was attractive, he had no difficulty in doing so.

The princesse de Bormes reopened her flat, disused because of the war, and redecorated it. She did not mix her pleasures. The pleasure of being

mistress of the house interfered with the pleasures
of heroism. She no longer followed the convoy
regularly, she only lent the car. She painted,
polished, varnished and made purchases. Guillaume had dinner in the avenue Montaigne almost
every day, apart from the trips.

These trips were growing much more compli-
cated. The services had become better organised,
and in France nothing seems so suspicious as not
to be on the records.

At the *troisième bureau* a few officers who had
escaped terrible dangers were received with a very
bad grace. *They were no longer on the records.*

This phantom convoy was annoying, but its
experiments were free. So it was not suppressed; it
had spokes put in its wheels.

Guillaume went on removing these spokes. The
hospital clung to him like a buoy.

They were watching General d'Ancourt's linger-
ing death in all its phases. They were afraid of an
end which would doubtless send his pseudo-secre-
tary back to the ranks.

One evening at six o'clock they were waiting for
Guillaume; now Headquarters gave the password
to him.

Guillaume had drunk punch after punch with cyclists from the Invalides. At the top of his voice he was proclaiming the word which France hides next to her heart, guarding it with her life.

Horrified, the comte d'Oronge, an old voluntary nurse, took Guillaume by the scruff of the neck and shook him. Guillaume, struggling to get free, called the old man a fool. The courtyard formed a ring, and no-one dared contradict the General's nephew.

At last, when the comte d'Oronge, pale with anger, had thrown Guillaume to the ground, Guillaume got up, shook his fist at Verne, and yelled, as he went out, that they would be hearing from him.

They tried to pacify the Count, who was mechanically repeating, "the rascal! the rascal!" And, as no-one had remembered the password in the confusion, the convoy could not set out.

When it was after eight o'clock, the doctor telephoned the princess. She was expecting Guillaume for dinner; he was not there.

This call drove the princess and Henriette frantic. They thought Guillaume was in the rue Jacob, and pictured him under a bus. At nine o'clock they

telephoned Verne. He told them nothing of the
scene, and simply said that Guillaume had come
and gone.

Pesquel-Duport, who was at dinner, chaffed
them; then, when he was alone with Clémence,
told her she was silly to become so worked up
about a schoolboy. Just who was he? Where did
he come from? Where on earth did he come from?

"Why," she exclaimed, "you know, I suppose,
what his name is?"

"What proof have you that that is his name?"
replied the Editor.

For the first time, Madame de Bormes, tongue-
tied, realized that she had no proper information
about Guillaume. But apart from the fact that his
success was as good as papers, she did not want to
give herself away.

"I know all I need to know about him," she
said. And, transforming a doubt that struck her
into a means of self-justification on the spur of the
moment, she added, "do you think, Editor, that I
ought to let all and sundry go about with
Henriette?"

Now while this dialogue was going on in the
avenue Montaigne, Guillaume, drunk as a school-

boy, was abandoning himself to what was without
doubt one of the most incomprehensible acts of his
career.

The alcohol had pushed open a flimsy door on
reality, and he hurried off to his aunt's to protest.

The good old woman could not understand his
protests. She gathered that Guillaume was being
tortured, that his stripe was being affronted in a
civilian hospital, and that Guillaume begged her
to tell everyone to respect him.

She mistook his maudlin tears for tears of shame,
and confused the small arms course, the liaison
service, and the hospital. Briefly, in the face of such
despair, she promised to go to the rue Jacob and
speak to Verne. Guillaume shut himself in his
room, and, without undressing, fell into a brute
sleep.

He was still asleep the following morning when
his aunt went down the rue Jacob.

By the time she had been sitting in the caretaker's room for a quarter of an hour, Verne had
grasped the real catastrophe, that Guillaume
Thomas was plain Thomas, and that he was
sixteen.

His Cross danced before his eyes like a cascading

artichoke of sparks at a firework display.

Hearing the doctor speak of her family the Fontenoys, of General de Fontenoy and of General de Fontenoy's nephew, the poor old maid cried, "But there is a mistake. A great mistake. Guillaume was born at Fontenoy, that is all. That is not his name. How could he? Oh! Oh!" And she had a fit.

Verne took stock of the situation quickly. He braced himself. It was important that Guillaume should stay what he was, or rather what he was not.

Verne held the old maid's hands and produced a deluge of fluid. Making a travesty of the mesmerizer's words, he almost shouted "You are Fontenoy, I will it."

She recovered her wits.

"Quietly, quietly," said Verne. "Drink a little water. There, there. Don't scold Guillaume. He has too fine a name to be scolded."

And as the old lady protested, "Hush, hush, hush," went the doctor, "I won't listen to you. I know, I know. You are too modest."

This preposterous word finished the good woman. The doctor froze her with a terrible stare and hustled her towards the door.

"And above all, not a word of our conversation

to your nephew," he said in a whisper. "Things of great moment depend on it. Swear it. Swear it on your missal," he cried, seizing the book which was poking out of a bag.

The unfortunate woman swore. She thought she was with a madman. She was not far wrong. The doctor was out of his mind with worry.

He escorted her to the arched gateway in case she met anyone. He was right. They passed the princess on her way in.

Verne watched the old spinster turn the street-corner. Madame de Bormes was waiting in the courtyard.

"Well, how silly I am!" he exclaimed. "Don't you know that excellent lady?"

And, as the princess looked vague, "That is Guillaume's aunt, Mademoiselle de Fontenoy."

*   *   *

No words could be dearer to Madame de Bormes. She congratulated herself on her replies to the Editor's insinuations.

"Journalists live on front page news," she thought.

Thomas woke up in his aunt's house with a headache and not the slightest recollection of the escapades of the previous night. He only remembered that the punch and exhaustion had stopped him undressing. He got ready and went down the Butte to the hospital.

The princess was sitting in Verne's room. He had just told her about the password scene, glossing over the rough bits. "Guillaume is rather impulsive . . . Monsieur d'Oronge is rather deaf. Guillaume had sent his aunt here with the idea of fighting a duel with me."

He laughed, trying to twist his great shark-like face into an expression of grandfatherly goodwill.

"Guillaume! Here's Guillaume!"

Madame de Bormes shrieked. They could see him through the glass door, standing among the cars.

"Bring him in," exclaimed the doctor, opening the door. "Bring in our prodigal child."

The doctor was divided between hatred and respect. He hated Guillaume for having fooled him, but he respected the manoeuvre. He must go shares in it. The rogue wa² in his hands and he could use him without taking risks. The princess would cover him.

Titles intoxicated Verne. He thought it would be in bad taste to quibble over a title with the princesse de Bormes, and that her authority in this world must be enough to christen a chicken a carp or a Thomas Fontenoy, if she should ever be challenged.

Incapable of reading the riddle of such a woman, he accused her of the worst, and did not stop at making her the young cheat's mistress.

The princess scolded Guillaume for his blunder of the previous night. He told her about the punch.

At the name of M. d'Oronge, everything came back to his mind like a shot.

"Because of you," said Verne, "the convoy is stuck and the casualties have been kept waiting. The cars should have left at midnight. They are still in the courtyard. By the way," he added casually, "I have had a visit from your aunt. A very devout person, like the General."

He cast a furtive glance at Guillaume. Guillaume took the remark as a matter of course.

Good Lord, thought Verne, the sly dog! He is tough. He'll go a long way, if he's not stopped first. We must see that he is not stopped until it is too late.

"Why don't I know your aunt?" asked Clémence.

"She's a saint," said Guillaume; "she never leaves her house except to go to the Sacré-Coeur. This morning she must have come because she was going down to Saint François-Xavier, where she burns candles."

The doctor nodded his head in silent applause, like the guilty man at a trial listening to an accomplice who never betrays himself. His mind was made up. He would not be Guillaume's fool any more. He would play him at his own game.

There are convincing and unconvincing people, there are those who win and those who lose. The doctor was a loser.

To Guillaume, the convoy, the first-aid party, Verne, Madame Valiche, the dentist, and the radiographer's wife were an empty vessel. The princess and Henriette were the contents.

We should write, Henriette and the princess, as, for some time, Guillaume had been troubled with the first signs of love, which overtakes a boy steal-

thily at first and makes him ugly, feeble and colour-
less, before appearing in its splendour. He was
flagging, torn apart by his physical growth, the
truth about himself, the part he was playing, and
the disturbances of normal development under a
heap of untruths.

Guillaume's lack of introspection and his active
day-dreaming did not help him to see clearly. By
trying to keep in the half-light, he let himself be
caught in the pitch-darkness. Instead of telling
himself that he loved Henriette, which was not a
part of his act, he riveted his attention on the act,
and attributed the disturbances to inactivity and
to the lack of adventures.

General d'Ancourt died. Guillaume grasped this
excuse to disappear from the hospital. Verne was
furious. But what could he do?

Without saying anything to the two women,
Guillaume went to see Pesquel-Duport at his
office. He made up the story that General
d'Ancourt's death gave him his freedom, that he
would be discharged because of his leg and his
nervous condition, that it was only through his
uncle that he had been able to follow the General,
that they had refused to take him in the belief that

this would please the General, who already had
more than one bereavement to bear. He was sick
of being in the rear, and begged him to send him
to one of the canteens which the newspaper ran at
the front. The avenue Montaigne must not hear a
thing about this move of his. He would pretend
to have had his orders.

Pesquel-Duport almost hugged him. Nothing
would suit him better than to have Guillaume at
a distance. He hid his satisfaction, cut him short,
congratulating him on his courage, and told him
that in return for a promise of absolute silence to
Madame de Bormes, he would enrol him in the
Coxyde canteen on the Belgian front.

The Belgian front was manned by Belgians,
Zouaves, riflemen, English and marines. There was
plenty of scope here. Guillaume beamed.

His exuberance was short-lived. Once again he
felt sad without knowing why. He dared not raise
his tear-filled eyes to Henriette and her mother.
Madame de Bormes thought he had taken his
master's death very much to heart. Love made
Henriette a Stradivarius, a barometer sensitive to
the slightest changes of mood. This sadness, which
Guillaume took for a combination of boredom and

remorse and Clémence for grief, was fully understood by Henriette alone.

This remorse was not related to a breach of
good form, which no longer was one in his eyes,
but to the fact that he had secretly asked the Editor
to send him away from the two women. At least,
this convenient reason gave him an explanation for
the state he was in.

And so it was with some embarrassment that he
told Madame de Bormes and her daughter of his
posting. The blow was less severe because of the
privileges of the post (an invalid's post, Guillaume
explained) and the coincidence which attached him
to a service organized by Pesquel-Duport.

But the princess knew by the affinity between
them that the safest post in the world would not
remain so for Guillaume.

"As long as you don't play the fool," she moaned.
"I shall warn the Editor to give orders to have
you watched."

The week of his departure, that was so short,
seemed endless.

While he thought he was escaping boredom on
the back of his chimera, Guillaume was forging a
link between these women and himself, the link

which strengthens as it grows longer, and inverts perspective, since people who are going away seem to grow out of all proportions.

Henriette could not sleep at night. She would tell herself, he loves me. He thinks I don't love him, or, he is afraid of mother. He's going away and he's suffering. She spelt out the alphabet of love unaided. It needed all the princess's anxiety, her ladders and her paintpots to hide her daughter's red eyes from her.

Tears and presents made Guillaume's departure tragi-comical. Afterwards Henriette fell ill.

"Henriette is like me," said Clémence to Pesquel-Duport. "She has always had her father's unbearable stability. But for some time she has been going to extremes, like me. This metamorphosis brings us closer together. She is ill because Guillaume has left. I am glad."

It was obvious that the girl was in love. As soon as Pesquel-Duport noticed it, he cast another weight overboard to join the one he had discarded when Guillaume left.

Alas! Watching her daughter blindly, Clémence did not see that it was like a lied by Heinrich Heine; Henriette was in love with a phantom.

71

Le Jour's canteen was camped on the road between Nieuport-ville and Coxyde-ville, dispensing provisions and pep to the relieving troops. It consisted of a smoking alchemists' waggon where the nine volunteers took turns at distributing pints of black coffee or punch at the roadside. These volunteers, who ranked with second lieutenants, supervised by a real second lieutenant, were billeted at Coxyde in a criminal's hut. All these huts were like dens of crime, particularly the tumbledown ones at Coxyde-bains. Old holiday cabins of Belgian bathers, they lined the North sea coast.

Seen from the air, Nieuport-ville, Nieuport-bains and Coxyde-ville made up a twisted framework of roads.

Between Coxyde-bains and Nieuport-bains were sand-dunes. Fields, farms, and a wood known as Triangular Wood lay between Coxyde-ville and Nieuport-ville. The countryside was empty—secretly packed with men.

The French and English artillery took advantage of the dunes and the trees. The Zouaves and the riflemen occupied the trenches at the mouth of the Yser, where one of their sentries guarded the first dip of this dug-out town that wound from one end of France to the other. Finally, on the Saint-Georges side, the marines kept watch over a strip of land that had been dearly won in the Battle of the Yser.

The Zouaves and the marines spent their time off together in the former houses and estates of Coxyde-bains.

The two Nieuports, in ruins, had nothing but the shelter of their cellars to offer the commanding officers and the first-aid posts of the different corps. The deserted towns and the countryside hid an incredible labyrinth of corridors, roads and underground galleries. Below, men moved about like moles and they could go in at a hole in Coxyde and come out by another on the front line without seeing the sky. Sector 131 was a quiet sector. An unwritten agreement stopped us firing on Ostend so that the enemy would not fire on La Panne, where the king and queen were exiled. The sovereigns lived there with the royal children, who were delighted by the surprise and the lovely farmyard.

The natural defenses of the river and the floods

shielded Nieuport from a real surprise attack.
None the less, the Colonel expected a night landing
from rafts on the beach. This was a chimerical
fear. He nurtured it. For that reason a communica-
tion trench had been dug along the coast between
Nieuport and the Yser, a pinewood trench redolent
of Swiss hotels, which bore the Colonel's name.
The Colonel thought his trench was one of the
wonders of the world—and not without reason.
In fact, it hung like the Gardens of Babylon, it was
as useless as the Pyramids, as hollow as the Colossus
of Rhodes, as gloomy as the tomb of Mausolus, as
costly as the statue of Jupiter, as cold as the temple
of Diana and as conspicuous as the lighthouse of
Alexandria. Look-outs occupied it and shot at
seagulls.

Underneath Nieuport it was like the théâtre du
Châtelet below the stage. They had connected the
cellars and nicknamed this conduit *Nord-Sud*.
Every entrance sported the name of a station on
the *Nord-Sud* line, and not the least of its pleasures
was to emerge at the sign *Concorde* set in the
middle of a ruined casino.

One branch led to the Colonel's cellar, the
command post. This cellar was part of the villa

Pas sans peine. The dining-room alone, by some miracle, had been left standing, and on quiet days the Colonel lunched there like a great rat in a chunk of Gruyère.

The sand-dunes were the show-piece of the sector.

This feminine landscape had its appeal. Smooth, curved, languorous, supine, it was alive with the activity of men. For the dunes only appeared to be deserted. In reality they were nothing but stage effects, scenery, sham, traps and contrivances. Colonel Quinton's imitation dune was a really feminine ruse. The gallant Colonel had built it under a hail of shells which fell on him as he sat smoking in a rocking-chair. There was a hidden observation post on top which the observer could vacate in a split second by sliding down on a toboggan.

In effect, these dunes which confronted the German telescopes looked like a great tower of cards or an untalkative card-sharper on the surface; on the reverse they had a never-ending supply of tricks.

"Where is the heavy gun? Where is she? On the right? On the left? In the middle? Follow me. Where is she? Right? Left? Bang! In the middle."

And under a dune-coloured canvas, like the dune with its camel's humps and a coat of pale grass, the gun recoiled and let fly a shell as heavy as a strongbox.

They could see nothing. They could hear the 155 m.m.'s and the 75 m.m.'s exploding like bottles of dry champagne, their shells like tearing silk, the English gun whose position they could never determine, the anti-aircraft guns that crown aeroplanes with little round clouds like the Virgin Mary's train of seraphim, the heaving North Sea, oyster-coloured, with its water that was so cold and grey, so like the formula H_2O $Na.Cl$ that you would have rather burnt yourself to death or buried yourself alive than have bathed in it.

The night, the sky and the earth shimmered in the light of the flares like a room in the candlelight when the flame flickers on the ceiling. If it was misty, the mist made the separate flashes of gunfire merge into one blinding, maddening flash. The searchlights embraced, parted and beckoned over the open sea. At times they came dancing together like ballerinas, and at their tips gleamed the white bellies of Zeppelins on their way to London.

Was there any sleep in Coxyde? The naval guns

broke it. The fire shook the earth, and cast a great convolvulus of mauve light on the window-panes.

On Sundays, with the machine-guns overhead shouting out the monotonous laughter of grinning skulls, and the engines whose droning would suddenly deepen from pale blue to black velvet, the officers of the Royal Navy played tennis.

*　　　　*　　　　*

It only needed Guillaume de Fontenoy to complete this illusory waste of sand and leaves.

*　　　　*　　　　*

He came. It was evening. A side car brought him from Dunkirk. The canteen gave him an icy reception. The reason was that Pesquel-Duport had seconded the life and soul of the section to make a place for Guillaume. Guillaume was usurping a place that was still warm; but it was such a cold place that it chilled him to the marrow. He expected to find friends. He found mortal enemies.

Impervious to Guillaume's magical charm, the stupid fellows thought him to be an accessory to a crime he knew nothing about, and sent him to Coventry. Only the General's name might have changed the attitude of these men, afraid of rank and on the look-out for preferment. But a sector is a provincial town where the chemist commands more respect than a medical specialist. Fontenoy was not in command of the sector.

The stupid bunch saw at once that Guillaume was enthusiastic. This was the last straw. Every volunteer was as unlike a volunteer as he could be. There was no bond of honour, cheerfulness or sincerity between them. They took Guillaume's enthusiasm as an insult.

He's setting us a challenge, they thought. And in revenge they sent him to take orders to the Zouaves in the danger-zone. This suited Guillaume perfectly. He strolled through a park of fire and thunder, in raptures.

It was in this way that he came to know Colonel Jocaste. The Colonel was staggered when he read the name de Fontenoy. He took Guillaume into his dug-out and, as it was five o'clock, asked him to tea. The telephonist played the daughter of the house. He set cups, a teapot, and a tin of biscuits on one end of the table.

78

As it was forbidden to loot the houses, and every single utensil came from that source, everyone always pretended to have found everything in the church.

"These cups came from the church," said the Colonel, winking.

The Colonel pestered Guillaume with questions about his uncle. The General was his god. As he talked he wound puttees round his fat legs, groaning as if they were bandages. He confided his fears about the rafts to Guillaume, and outlined his plan of defence. He was also afraid of gas, which was almost out of the question in this region where the winds were always changing. He was proud of his dining-room with its lace hangings.

"I'm afraid I never give up the conventions, if I can help it. I'm mad about them. And so, between you and me I have a mistress, a society woman. Whenever she dines alone with me, or with her husband and myself, its always a low dress for her and dinner jackets for the men."

His fourth obsession was a 75 m.m. in the front line, thirty yards from the enemy listening post, that had been assembled there bolt by bolt, like a ship in a bottle.

"Won't they look sick?" he often said, "if there's
an attack. A 75 m.m. in the front line!"

Then he would laugh and slap his thighs.

Suddenly the door opened and the General in
command of the sector appeared.

With two captains plastered with straps and
ribbons, he was holding an inspection, a sort of
surprise-party that was most unpleasant for the
recipients.

The Colonel leapt to his feet, bowed, and
knocked over the tin of dry biscuits. A social reflex
made the General bend down to pick them up, and
as he did so, he bumped his helmet against the
head of the Colonel who was bending over the
other way.

"Have I hurt you?" he asked.

He had hurt him badly. The Colonel replied
that he had not. From a corner of the cellar
Guillaume absorbed this surprising scene.

Now the poor Colonel, partially recovered from
the physical and mental shock, was describing his
wonders.

He had got on to his 75 m.m. in a hut, and the
General, doubtless forgetting the camouflage of the
dunes, was asking if the hut was screened with

leaves, when a gunner appeared. The Colonel waved him away, but the General protested, stressing that on no account would he interrupt the normal work of the sector.

"What is it?" said the Colonel.

It was about the 75 m.m. After an endless introduction, the man got round to saying that the genius' measurements were wrong, that the hut was too small and the gun-carriage could be seen, and that it looked as if the enemy might make a party of the reprisals.

"Reprisals! Reprisals!" burst out the Colonel, angry at being made to look ridiculous in front of the General. "We shall see. I'll give them reprisals."

"Fire a hundred rounds with the 75 m.m. on the Vromberg house," he shouted down a speaking tube.

"Vromberg?" asked the General. "Of course," he said turning to one of his captains, "that was Madame Vromberg's house. A charming woman. Poor Madame Vromberg."

"Do you know her Sir?" cried the Colonel, losing his head. And, grabbing the speaking-tube, "Cancel the firing order," he said. "Can-cel-the-firing-or-der."

The General saw what a state the good man was in as a result of his visit.

"Heavens, now you are being chivalrous over ruins," he said. "I am going. It looks as if everything is running as smoothly as it could be. Stay here. Don't disturb yourself. Don't bother. I know the way."

The colonel found himself alone with Guillaume. He was perspiring freely. He rubbed a bruise caused by the helmet. He wondered if he had seemed to be up to the mark.

"Of course, there is the business of the 75 m.m.," he kept on saying. "But my tube cancels all that."

They had tea.

*　　　*　　　*

Bureaucrats and more bureaucrats, thought Guillaume. He was looking for a breach. The place of terror where he could hear the night exploding like a mass of fireworks, the gunfire as sharp and irregular as the twitches of a man dreaming that he is walking while he is asleep, this was his goal.

Two days later, the Colonel gave him a guide to visit the lines. They left by moonlight, at eleven o'clock.

Instead of using the trench system so dear to the Colonel, they disobeyed him and went up the old main street of Nieuport to the parapet. They walked from strongpoint to strongpoint between dominoes of shadow, cast by a few walls, and of moonlight. The moonlight gave stature to these young ruins, and to the right of the sand two or three trees, drugged with chloroform, stood sleeping.

A bridge made of beams, joists, planks, logs and barrels jostling against one another spanned the Yser at its mouth. The grey water thrust its tragic way into the North Sea, like a herd of sheep going into the slaughter-house.

At night, the water was phosphorescent. A cartridge-case thrown into it went down like the Titanic, in a blaze of light. As it sank, a shell would light up an avenue of dazzling shops on the river-bed.

The trenches began on the other bank. Guillaume touched the first of the sandbags that protect the dug-out town, where bullets bury themselves humming like bees in a flower.

The maze of trenches was endless. Guillaume followed his silent guide who was smoking a pipe, wrapped in mitts, sheepskins, and Balaclava helmets. They could hear the water, now behind them, now in front, to left or to right. They went round in circles without realizing it, and never knew where the sea was. Sometimes they were knee-deep in water.

This dream-Venice, Algiers or Naples seemed as empty as the dunes, for, in hundreds of cellars, the Zouaves were asleep, packed like bottles. They cracked them when they ran riot.

The meandering German and French lines almost met in two places on the front. The first, near Saint-Georges, was called Mamelon-Vert, the second was near the beach. Both sides had dug listening posts there.

Guillaume slid into the sap. There was only room to wriggle along the ground. The sap led into a trench occupied by two men. During the day they played cards. The enemy held a similar trench twelve yards away. Whenever one of the Zouaves sneezed, a German voice called out, "God bless you!"

The look-outs stood along the parapet of the
front line on a sort of embankment, cornice or
pedestal. A bit of everything had gone to build the
wall, like the rest of the town. Apart from sandbags, it seemed to be made of ice-boxes, chests of
drawers, armchairs, piano lids, of dullness, despon-
dency, and silence.

The silence, heightened by the gun-fire and the
ebb-tide, was like the silence of snow falling in a
glass ball. Walking here was like flying in a dream.

Guillaume's rubber boot slipped and splashed
in the water. One of the look-outs turned round.
He was an Arab scout. He put his finger to his
lips. Then he became a statue again.

For this Arab, his newspaper burnous tied on
with string, was as motionless as the dead Antar on
his horse. Through the bags, floury with moonlight,
Guillaume studied this silhouette of a fierce and
jealous miller watching with a gun at the window
of his mill.

All the life in these look-outs was concentrated
in their figures. When they were reloading, their
hands darted to and fro like domestic servants.
And so France had an amazing ermine border of
attentive faces around her cloak.

But what attracted Guillaume was the stormy land, the common land overgrown with the thorns of barbed wire. No-one sets foot there when there is no attack, except on night patrols. Guillaume would have done anything in the world to be in one of the patrols.

Instead of that, he turned back. He was only a tourist. He walked out of the theatre into the street without taking part in the mysterious life of the actors.

*   *   *

He was immensely bored. Every week hung heavy on his hands. His only pleasure was in the letters and presents which Henriette and her mother sent him.

The unexciting days he passed made him fall back on his memories of the two women. Very slowly, like people who can only read at a distance, Guillaume made out his feelings for Henriette. She was far-off, unreal, fictitious. So she could become part of his fairy-tale.

He played this act magnificently. He sighed,

fumed, did not eat, cut hearts in aluminium rings, and wrote letters which he tore up afterwards. For with the velvet paws of cats playing with one another, knowing exactly how far their claws sink in, Guillaume, suffering all the pangs of love, did nothing to suggest it to Henriette, or to give the slightest substance to his dream.

He did not want to know if his love was reciprocated. He could say with Goethe: — *I love you; what is that to you?*

*   *   *

In the meantime the canteen had orders to move to the Somme. They left equipment in Belgium with a voluntary guard.

The volunteer appointed could only have been Guillaume. The fools thought they were doing him a bad turn in getting rid of him. In fact, they were getting him rid of them.

Two days after they had left, Guillaume met young Captain Roy of the marines.

"What, have they left you on your own?" he said. "Then come to our mess."

Heroism brought a miscellany of men together under one palm. Plenty of potential murderers found opportunities there and a reward for their vice, side by side with the martyrs. It is surprising that the *Joyeux*, the punishment battalion, for example, should have been brought into the war. They held the sector between the marines and the Zouaves. Society now approved of them giving rein to the instincts for which she had banished them.

But neither the Zouaves nor the marines took advantage of the license to shoot. There was no streak of brutality in the marines.

Their commanders were attractive, heroes. The bravest young men in the world, they are all gone. They played at fighting, without a hint of hatred. But games of this sort have bad endings.

They relieved each other at the lines and lived in a house in Coxyde-bains. Guillaume's good points captivated them. And really, how could he be reproached at this time? He was not deceiving anyone. It was not a General's name that impressed these great souls. In any case, the name lost its practical value in this place and became a simple *nom de guerre*. They all had them. Guillaume Thomas was Fontenoy just as Roy was Phantomas, Pajot, Giraffe-neck, Combescure, Sudden Death, Breuil de la Payotte, the Admiral's son, Admiral, and Le Gannec, Gordon Pym.

Their duty seemed to be the same as Madame de Bormes': to avoid boredom as much as possible. The rest of the sector could not understand it, as people failed to understand Clémence.

Their breezy manner was mistaken for snobbishness. They were considered to be aristocrats, which was not far from the truth. This battalion was an aristocracy, that is a solid democracy, a family.

The reception which they gave Guillaume would have been possible nowhere else. Jealousies, fear of the records, rank, or class differences, would have prevented it.

The battalion behaved with the lack of ceremony that is true elegance. After the meal, Le Goff, a sailor who waited at table, sewed anchors onto the dark blue canteen jacket, and the trick was done. Guillaume was adopted. They would never leave him.

The marines, like the princess, gave Guillaume

a home. They doted on him, they fêted him, and they asked his advice. They took him to dinner with their commanding officer. This charming old man thought the adoption just as funny as if his children, as he called his subalterns, had brought him a little bear. The fact is that like bears, monkeys and marmots, Guillaume had become a mascot. He felt that he had reached his goal. His love for Henriette dwindled. His emotions had been roused by her, but his love was just plain love. He turned it on to his new friends in all its force. He gave them the fruits of it. He was in love with the battalion.

*   *   *

Guillaume had everything in his favour, for if he had been a real marine, he would have had a hard time of it. As he had become a marine without being one, he could savour his happiness to the full.

He did not read the thick missives from the avenue Montaigne properly. He forgot about some, and left them unopened in his pocket. He passed the delicacies round the mess, and conveyed his thanks on postcards which limit one's effusions.

Had he the time to write? He was always follow-ing Roy or Breuil or Le Gannec to their posts. He went up to the lines with them, and was some-times bequeathed to their successor.

He had written one long letter; to Pesquel-Duport. He asked him to leave him at Coxyde, as the vague equipment provided an excuse for his endless stay.

His delight was so great that he tore up his permit. He told the mess that he could not make up his mind to leave. This was his crowning triumph. The young officers organized a dinner for him and had champagne bought at La Panne where the Hotel Terlinck and the bakery were still operating in spite of the bombs.

They got drunk and gave speeches. The name de Fontenoy was mentioned frequently, but with no great respect. To them the General was an old fogey, not an idol. The real idol being Guillaume Thomas.

*   *   *

Mademoiselle de Bormes and the princess were

living in the expectation of his leave. They thought out many treats for him, and Henriette's colour came back. The disappointment hit them hard. Guillaume said he could not leave the equipment. I would be robbed, he wrote.

This did not deceive them, but they were only to be worse deceived.

"He feels we are stopping him from going back to his duty," burst out Clémence.

In her bed a tearful Henriette kissed a snapshot sent by Guillaume, repented of her silence, and, in a flood of emotion, was tortured with fears, from the idea that Guillaume did not love her and was running away from her to the idea that he did love her and wanted to smother a passion which he thought he could not hope to consummate.

She saw only these two alternatives, black and white. She could see nothing between them.

The optimism of her age made her incline towards the white.

He loves me, she thought, and his sense of good form is keeping him away. He is afraid of being taken for a seducer, or of mother sending him away. I alone am guilty. My listlessness is giving him away.

Henriette decided to speak and plead. But she

could not bring herself to do it. Her secret was so dear to her that she shrank from sharing it with anyone.

Frantic, the two women besieged Pesquel-Duport. Everything was his fault. They could not talk so well.

No matter how he exonerated himself, and explained discipline in the services, the avenue Montaigne was beginning to be a curse to him.

Then he had one of the flashes of inspiration which make journalists' fortunes when they are directed at the public.

"The newspaper is organising performances of plays for the forces," he told the two women. "I am having the next performance in the North, I'll enrol you in the company, and come along myself."

The princess kissed him. Henriette wept.

The Editor kept his promise. Four days later Clémence, Henriette and he went off on the train to join the tour.

To the two women it felt like an excursion train taking them to a picnic. Guillaume knew nothing of it. The surprise lay ahead of him.

The company, recruited from divers sources, consisted of a few supers, a singer in a dress and a hat like a duchess, a famous tragic actor, a beginner in mourning, Certificate of Merit from the *Conservatoire* the previous year, and a juvenile lead whose son, a Colonel, had just won his seventh decoration. He was counting on seeing him at the front.

Pesquel-Duport was introducing the travelling companions to each other when the princess, astounded, saw Madame Valiche on her way back from buying oranges. She was wearing the costume described at the farm.

"Of all things!" exclaimed the horrible woman, "you! You here! But whatever has happened, *my dear*?"

The princess gave her the benefit of the "my dear," for she saw the world through rose-coloured spectacles and did not want to spoil anyone's pleasure. She introduced Pesquel-Duport, and said that she owed the favour to him, adding, "Guillaume Fontenoy is at Coxyde; we are hoping to see him there."

Go on with you, thought Madame Valiche, winking.

The princess did not want Madame Valiche, armed with their common memories, to trail after Guillaume and herself. At first she had hoped to hide their real purpose. She saw at once that the woman would retaliate by detecting some mystery. This system of thought led her to make the simple statement—with some embarrassment.

Pesquel-Duport was astute, but not astute enough. He noticed Clémence's tone of voice and the wink.

He disliked both.

Now Madame Valiche was explaining:—

"You are going to clap me, *my dear*. I wanted to see the North. Romuald, my instructor" (she indicated the tragic actor) "is taking me with him. But wait, I am paying my way. I am *giving La Fiancée du Timbalier*, just think of that. And I am in *La Fille du Tambour-Major*."

The princess introduced Henriette, who thought she was already at the play. In the uninhibited way of the young, she laughed openly at Madame Valiche and the actors, went on smiling broadly and studied them as if they were strange animals.

Pesquel-Duport had had the foresight to reserve a compartment for the two women and himself, some distance away from the compartment where the company was.

Every time Madame Valiche passed by along the corridor, she eyed the empty places and conveyed in mime through the windows, "my word! You're not badly off in there!" which was a reproach. For they were packed tight in their compartment.

The princess was writhing. Pesquel-Duport stuck it out.

"Don't ask her in," he said. "The woman's like a fly-paper."

When Pesquel-Duport went to say a few kind words to his flock, he heard the great Romuald telling the story of the 1870 war. He was telling it from the beginning. The month before, he had had an idea which would astound anyone who does not know theatre life.

He had been the first to hear of the heroic death of one of his pupils, and had gone to see the parents, a good couple who worshipped their son. Thinking to break the news gently, he had recited it to them in the form of a sonnet of his own composition.

The unhappy pair were at dinner. Romuald began to recite at the door. They did not under-

stand, and thought he was mad. He had to explain
to them afterwards, and it was like coming down
with the axe a second time after missing the
criminal's head once.

The young actress in mourning was this pupil's
fiancée. She knew the sonnet by heart.

Cars were waiting for them at Dunkirk. The
tragic actor wore a stove-pipe hat, a leather pouch,
and binoculars. He was looking for enemy planes.

*   *   *

The following morning at La Panne where the
company was staying, Madame de Bormes and her
daughter, hopping with excitement, almost fainted;
for Guillaume, Roy and Pajot, hearing that
actresses had arrived, had come to meet them.

Guillaume thought he was dreaming when he
saw who the actresses were. This was ample proof,
for him, that he was not dreaming. The women
and he made a group like an Empire painting: —
The Soldier's Return.

Light-hearted and jubilant, Guillaume received
them with open arms. He had been unable to make

the effort of going to them, but he was overjoyed that they should come to him and meet his friends. His was not one of these narrow, suspicious minds that like to keep things in water-tight compartments.

A miracle which lasts ceases to be considered a miracle. That is why ghosts disappear so quickly.

A quarter of an hour later, no-one was surprised any more. Guillaume kissed Madame Valiche, and the marines bore the Editor and the two ladies away.

They would join the company that night at Coxyde for the play.

It was raining. For these three people, it was the most beautiful day of their lives. Pesquel-Duport seemed years younger, and the marines liked him.

Madame de Bormes and Henriette availed themselves of the preparations made for the actresses, and fancied that they were to have a fairy-tale reception. They took inordinate delight in the dunes, aeroplanes, guns and helmets, and in going indoors through the kitchen, where half-naked devils tattooed with anchors bobbed up and down around the cooking-pots, in the light of a hellish fire.

Madame de Bormes was an amazing success. All these men risked being killed the next day, and they surrendered themselves whole-heartedly, without a second thought. The warm atmosphere which surrounded her, like Guillaume, added to her attractions.

And a beautiful woman and a blooming girl are striking against this sort of scenery, like roses on an ice-floe.

Roy took them everywhere. They were greeted with cheers. The men kissed their hands and touched their dresses. Everyone saw the likeness of their loved ones in them.

Madame de Bormes, who could scent the ridiculous from a distance, felt that without being ridiculous she could and *should* tear the leather fringe off her coat and distribute the pieces. Seldom does a woman find herself in the position to make such a gesture. The queen of Belgium could not have been a greater success.

Guillaume was proud of her and watched Henriette. In such rich and favourable conditions Henriette did not call her happiness into question.

99

And so she gave the reins to her enjoyment, and was not afraid of looking frivolous to Guillaume.

This gentle slope led them to the play.

*   *   *

The play took place in a shed belonging to the English squadron, better equipped than our elegant stages.

The commanders' cars purred, their lights out. Men brought the cards out of their pockets. The soldiers went in one by one, for as the hall was quite small the places had been allotted with a sparing hand.

The unlucky ones were philosophical about it. Sitting on the sand, they listened to a comrade reciting monologues. Others made holes in the boards with their bayonets to see the actresses undressing.

The orchestra played the national anthems of the Allies from beginning to end. They became more and more animated as they went on. Then the French, English and Belgian generals sat down, and the show began.

The company performed *La Peur des Coups*, one

act of *L'Etincelle*, and one act of *La Fille du Tambour-Major*.

As the first of these plays is about a captain, and captains appear in the following ones, the soldiers thought it was a three-act play. They could not grasp the plot.

After the plays and the operetta, with Madame Valiche dressed up as a drummer, she appeared on the stage alone, and recited *La Fiancée du Timbalier* in this immodest costume. She was very popular.

She managed to give the poem a spicy, topical flavour by her facial expressions and hints. The singer was less popular. She tried to make the audience join in a marching song that soldiers never sing, and her cries of "all together, chaps," fell on deaf ears.

Romuald saved the stakes by declaiming the Marseillaise with a tricolour flag draped over his shoulder.

*　　*　　*

After the performance, the company was invited

to General Madelon's quarters. Madame de Bormes
and her daughter could not stay away, particularly
as Pesquel-Duport was to be present in his official
capacity.

Guillaume and his friends agreed that when they
came out, the trio should meet them and they
would take them secretly to Saint-Georges; the
General forbade them to take civilians to see the
lines.

The General, who had misunderstood Pesquel-
Duport's name, and thought he was not a newspaper editor but the theatre manager, congratulated him on his company.

"You have an excellent company there," he told
him.

"I am a guest, Sir," Pesquel-Duport mildly
corrected him.

"Good Lord, so am I! So am I! And I don't
complain, hang it! Do I, ladies?" cried the General.

His expression was meaningless. He called expressions like this 'the right spirit.'

The princess and Henriette were only waiting
to go. Pesquel-Duport frowned. At last, at the
permitted time-limit, they left.

"Good, very good indeed, ladies!" said the

General, who recognized them as the performers in *L'Etincelle*.

*   *   *

The rest of the night was sublime.

Although their shoes got caught between the duckboards, the two women went on walking for four hours.

In a cellar at Nieuport, Guillaume had enveloped them in great-coats and helmets.

On the way back they were dropping with exhaustion.

Once the princess came to a halt.

"I don't know what's the matter with me, but I feel shaky," she said.

"You're not afraid, are you? Keep low, and don't be frightened," said Roy. "The enemy is asleep."

"It is stupid. I am a silly thing. Let's go on."

*   *   *

Madame Valiche either knew of the trip to the

lines or she guessed at it. She was furious not to
have been taken, and she paid them back for it.

On the return journey she took advantage of
being alone with Henriette in the corridor, and
thinking that her mother and Guillaume were
having an affair, she transfixed the girl and pretended to look round to see if anyone could over-
hear them. She whispered.

"Listen . . . Guillaume is mad about you . . .
Look out. Don't drive the little fellow to despair.
He might go and get his brains blown out."

And without waiting for a reply she left Henriette tongue-tied and frozen to go back to the
actor's compartment.

*   *   *

In the mess the two women were the sole topic
of conversation. They contributed more to Guillaume's prestige than an uncle who was a General.

"That youngster worships you, you know," Roy
told him.

In the tone of voice he had used before, in
Verne's room to answer the princess, my aunt's a
saint, etc., Guillaume replied.

"It's reciprocal. We love each other like brother and sister."

For this visit had brought something of value to Guillaume and left it with him. He had a new piece of equipment for his strange game. Henriette could go to the ends of the earth and he would lose nothing by it.

*   *   *

A misfortune fell on the Coxyde section.

Pajot was due to go on leave the day he left the lines. So he was trembling all night in case there should be an accident. Roy teased him, and when Pajot begged him to keep quiet he cast a pool of light on his face with his pocket torch. Pajot fell stone dead, a bullet through his head. The bullet was a stray one, but Roy considered himself a murderer. He fell into the deepest despair.

Guillaume did not leave him; he watched him and tried to raise his spirits.

*   *   *

Mademoiselle de Bormes, in Paris, could not

forget Madame Valiche's words. She had stopped resenting that a woman of that sort should intrude on her distress. She reproached herself with committing a crime.

Had she not loved Guillaume, her duty alone almost forced her to pretend that she did; and she was in love with him.

She took a very wise course; to confide in Pesquel-Duport.

She arranged that they should go together to meet her mother who was seeing what the golf was like at Saint-Cloud.

In the car, pale, more dead than alive, she laid her heart bare.

Pesquel-Duport knew that she was smitten, but not as badly as that.

Enquiries had just confirmed, the night before, that although Guillaume was of an excellent family, he was usurping the name de Fontenoy. He found himself in a very difficult position. Faced with this lavish display, the good man decided to suspend judgment. He told Henriette that he would speak to her mother, and begged her to calm down, to have faith in him.

"Act quickly," shrieked the girl like an old

harridan. "We haven't a moment to lose. Save him!"

She blew her nose, pushed back her hair, and put her hat straight; and Pesquel-Duport thought of his own love, of his age, of Clémence, almost as blooming as Henriette.

She says that she will never fall in love again, he thought. Perhaps she has never been in love yet. I think she is younger than her daughter, much younger.

The car drove on. Silent, Henriette turned a haggard face to the landscape.

Pesquel-Duport went on to himself; of course, there is her enthusiasm for Guillaume. But when these things are serious, they are hidden. Still, she is such a novice that she is capable of being in love without knowing it, of becoming aware of it even more slowly than her daughter.

He wondered what was the best policy.

He worked out this plan.

The plan was in execrable taste, harsh and fraught with danger. But he was in love, and love does not carry much sense of propriety, gentleness or security with it.

He would tell Clémence that her daughter was

in love with Guillaume, and persuade her to give
her to him. By this means he would see the effect
of the news, for one thing, and whether she took
it as a mother or a rival; for another, he would
not commit her far, because as a last resort, the
discovery of Guillaume's false name and his age
would break the engagement. The Editor was
counting on this well-judged *coup de théâtre* to
cure Henriette.

*　　*　　*

That very evening a friend who was at dinner
with them went to a concert and left them alone.
Pesquel-Duport put his plan into operation.

"Heavens! The fool!" cried the princess. "She
is in love and she's hiding it. Why, I'm amazed,
Editor. And Guillaume is in love with her? What
a lucky thing! When I think how I could marry
Bormes. Am I so stupid, so unobservant? Well
. . . I deserve all the reproach I get."

Pesquel-Duport could not get over it. The
woman would always baffle him.

Her ebullience made him apply the brakes. He
protested that they would have to wait, make

enquiries, that chance . . .

"Chance!" broke in the princess. "Don't worry. First of all, who says that Guillaume is poor? The Fontenoys are rich. I shall make a proper settlement on Henriette. Besides," (she burst out laughing) "we're losing our heads, my poor Editor. We're a pair of fools. Here we are talking seriously about something that doesn't exist. Henriette knows nothing about anything. Guillaume is nineteen. He's the first boy she has met. She thinks she is in love with him. She isn't. Why, I'm in love with Guillaume too. But its not love."

The princess assumed a solemn manner to make these fantastic statements. With a wave of the hand she stopped Pesquel-Duport opening his mouth.

As he listened to her, he felt his fears return.

"I do not want to marry Henriette without due consideration," went on Clémence, "nor to give Guillaume a wife who will be tired of him in a fortnight. You can picture me with a son-in-law on my hands.""

The word son-in-law, applied to Guillaume, sent her off into another fit of laughter.

She's mad, thought Pesquel-Duport seriously, but I'm mad about her.

When she had stopped laughing, the princess asked him for the details. The Editor became confused, and toned down the scene in the car.

"Why, you're no good for anything but writing articles," said Clémence. "Be quiet. I shall use a very simple method. I shall ask Henriette."

She rose and disappeared.

Pesquel-Duport buried his head in his hands. He had a firm hold on life; but he had tears in his eyes. Of what use was this hold to him? He could not grasp Clémence. She glided, span round, and melted away. He felt that she was unreal, insubstantial. He kept on saying to himself, I am in love with a mad woman, a fairy. Does she love Guillaume? No. She loves no-one. She doesn't love herself. She doesn't love her daughter. She is neither a flirt nor a mother. She has another destiny which is beyond my understanding.

It is even simpler than that. She is just fickle, impossibly fickle. Is she in love with Guillaume without knowing it? Then I should have a chance. Perhaps she is in love with me without knowing it. Perhaps she is in love with both of us.

Pesquel-Duport was wandering, stumbling and going round in circles.

The fire made him doze off. When he awoke, he looked at the time.

The princess had gone to see Henriette at eleven o'clock. It was one o'clock in the morning. He thought he had been waiting five minutes. For grief, doubt, and even a fire in the hearth distort all time.

Pesquel-Duport was a close enough friend in the avenue Montaigne to break the conventions. He went to listen at the girl's door, heard sobs, knocked, and entered.

Madame de Bormes was sitting on the bed. Mother and daughter were in each other's arms, weeping.

"Come in! Come in quickly!" cried the princess. "Tell this love-sick child that she shall have her Guillaume, that she will be his wife, I promise."

*   *   *

As the visit to the North front became more and more remote, the princess grew bored.

Her daughter saved her.

The day after the confession she seemed five.

years younger than the night before.

Henriette kissed her, hugged her, and admired this model mother who, far from preaching and dampening the ardour of youth, gave it new impetus.

After an endless discussion with both women expressing their opinion, it was decided that Henriette should write to Guillaume. The princess thought it normal for women to take the first steps.

She would add a post-scriptum to the letter to remove any impression of secrecy.

"Don't worry, I won't read it," she told Henriette.

Henriette locked herself in her room, looked at Guillaume's portrait and wrote: —

'My dear Guillaume,

I do not know how to begin this letter. I would like it to be a very short one, because I am not clever and what I have to say is very simple. My dear Guillaume, do nothing rash; I love you *too*.

I do not mean I love you in the way mother loves you, nor in the way I love mother. I am in love with you. It makes me ill and very happy. But I am afraid.

I gathered from your genuine pleasure when we came to La Panne that you were keeping away from the house out of a sense of good form. For if you had been running away from us for any other reason, the surprise would have been an unpleasant one.

My dear Guillaume, mother and I were glad to hear the soldiers speak well of you, but I do not need them to know you.

I am afraid you may be taking more risks than you are asked to, and putting your life in danger a dozen times while others do it once.

I am writing this difficult letter—which hurts me so much because I would rather speak to you and hold your hand—because I would like you to save yourself for me, for us, for our future. Mother is kinder than you can imagine. She allowed me to write to you and told me to write quickly to save time.

My dear Guillaume, write to me. Tell me if you love me as I love you, and if you are glad that mother is willing for us to be happy together.

I must go because I feel like crying and I should say the same thing over and over again. I send you my love, my dear Guillaume.'

Without reading the letter, the princess added at the foot of the page—

"You ought to be ashamed of yourself."

*   *   *

At six o'clock in the evening, as soon as Pajot had been buried, his canteen was in order, and the statement had been drawn up, Roy and Guillaume went back up to the line to relieve Combescure, who had been standing in for Roy for twenty-four hours.

They made the journey on foot, as the car which could have taken them to the bridge at Nieuport had had its engine destroyed by shrapnel near Triangular Wood.

The walk was less trying for Roy than if he had been with his men. He was walking as if he were out for a stroll, not loaded with weights like a greasy pole. But his load was of a different nature. His heart was heavier than the equipment.

Yet deaths were of no consequence in the sector.

Although a civilian death is the common lot, it keeps its prestige.

Death can even award a certificate of good life and good behaviour. People cannot help thinking, well! The man has just died. He is dead for all that. So he was not just anyone. Perhaps he was a better man than he seemed to be.

But at the lines, as if the prevalence of death, wounds and continual risks made every man die more than once, death was converted into small change and lost its value.

The rate of exchange was incredibly low.

So the dialect of the sector seemed brutal to those who came from the land-of-few-deaths.

Indeed, no-one said, "poor so and so," but "he could easily have taken cover."

They spoke of shells as if they were dangers of Paris that a short-sighted man or a provincial cannot avoid.

Pajot's death was an exception to the rule. The marines' house had lost a limb, and Roy was indirectly the cause of the loss.

"I killed him, as if my torch were a gun," he kept on saying.

So Guillaume and Roy walked on in silence. In the little night-lights that cap telegraph poles like lily-of-the-valley, the wind blew up the embers of its lament.

Roy, whose mother was a Breton, was superstitious. He could hear Pajot's spirit moaning.

He held tightly on to Guillaume, squeezed his arm, and bit his lip, like a child trying not to cry.

To return to Saint-Georges was to return to the scene of the crime. He was thankful for the accident to the car which delayed the event.

No matter how Guillaume argued coincidence, spent bullets, the difficulty at aiming at a head when it was only visible for a second, Roy persisted in his remorse.

"His family, his poor family," he muttered. "He was going to see his family. He begged me not to play the fool. It's really horrible."

*   *   *

Suddenly an extraordinary noise broke out in the darkness. It was the military band of the negro riflemen. They were passing through Coxyde-ville.

The band was composed of a native flute that soldiers imitate by holding their noses, striking a high note, and tapping their Adam's apple. This nasal flute can only play a high-pitched funereal tune. It sounds like the voice of Jezebel. The drums and bugles answered it.

116

Like the Ark of the Covenant on the road to Jerusalem, the troop drew nearer. Roy and Guillaume stood back and watched it pass.

The negroes, numb with cold and exhaustion, had come from Dunkirk. They were covered in shawls, mantillas, mittens, bags, mess-tins, cartridges, guns, the spoils of battle, charms, glass bead necklaces and bracelets of teeth.

The lower half of them was marching; the upper half was dancing to the music. It kept them going, it stimulated them. Their heads, arms, shoulders and bellies swayed, soothed by this savage opium. Out of step, their feet dragged in the mud. The silences were broken by the sound of their feet crunching into the mud and their rifle-butts knocking against their gas-mask cases; then, from the depths of the desert, from the depths of time, came the solo, ushered in by the brass and the drums.

Guillaume liked the band; it chilled the blood of his companion. Its wailing dirge was in keeping with his mourning. He remembered his travels with Pajot, their ship, their ports of call, their gay times in Eastern ports.

They resumed their walk without exchanging a word.

Triangular Wood was reverberating like a Royal
Chase. At Nieuport, the marines' cemetery lay near
the shapeless church. Beyond Nieuport, from the
trench which ran to Saint-Georges, the shell of a
farm could be seen rising above the floods, to the
right. It was called *Vache-Crevée*.

The originator of this nickname, used on the
ordnance survey maps, was a young Englishwoman,
Miss Elizabeth Hart.

Miss Hart, whom everyone called Elizabeth, was
the daughter of the General in command of the
English troops in the sector.

In the name of the Red Cross she piloted a
pocket ambulance and lived with the marines.

In a French woman, this sort of behaviour would
be shocking. But Elizabeth Hart was a real tomboy,
a minx. She dressed almost like a sailor. Short curly
hair framed her angelic face.

She was like the modern Amazons of the Ameri-
can cinema in more ways than one, except that she
was never seen to tremble. She went to and fro
between La Panne and the lines and parked her
ambulance wherever she fancied, as if the lines
were the streets of London. Her jauntiness antagon-
ized the Zouaves' colonel. He thought she was

uninhibited. So she neglected the sea-sector for the flood-sector.

The marines looked upon her as a saint.

Without any doubt, she was a heroine. The essentials of heroism being free-will, disobedience, the absurd and the unusual.

What is more, she could read hands.

*   *   *

When Guillaume and Roy reached Saint-Georges, she was sitting in Roy's dug-out drinking port with Combescure. She had just come back from a long leave. She did not know Guillaume. She spoke with an attractive accent.

She was careful how she pronounced our 'r's, and as she could not make them in her throat, she rolled them on the tip of her tongue. She told Roy he was silly to have scruples.

Combescure wanted her to read Guillaume's hand.

A truthful palmist had a difficult job at the front. She tried to back out of it. Guillaume was insistent.

When she looked at the palm of his hand, such

119

an expression of surprise came over her face that Combescure and Roy asked her the reason.

"Well! I've never seen a hand like that," replied Elizabeth. "He has several lines of life, not one."

"And what about my death . . . or my deaths?" asked Guillaume.

"I'm not very good at this, you know," she said. "I see it as a whole. On the whole, yours is good."

Combescure and Miss Hart left. She drove him to Coxyde.

"What a woman! She's marvellous!" said Guillaume to Roy.

"Another victim to Elizabeth. We've lost count of her dead," said the young captain with a smile. "She's plucky, and she's a good sort, which is worth a great deal more."

He did not want to talk. Guillaume sensed it. When Roy's orders had been given, he suggested a game of cards.

*   *   *

Captain Roy's dug-out was the only one in Saint-Georges that was fit to live in.

The water made it almost impossible to dig the ground. It gave the marines an excuse for their crazy recklessness.

Their trench system compared as unfavourably with the Zouaves' as a tree-trunk hive with a bee-keeper's.

There was no protection there from water or from fire.

This recklessness, in men used to the sway of the swell and their hammocks—even, when they had not been to sea, of their group spirit—was increasing because of the fact that an hour's bombing destroys five weeks' work.

Often, after an attempted German attack, the Zouaves suffered less from their wounds than from architects' pride.

Purely out of affection for their commanders, the marines had built a hut, with the remarkable touch of dressmakers who can turn a beret with a red pompom into a dream of elegance, and tie a knot like lovers' monograms.

So this segment was very dangerous and a lot of men were lost there.

Roy wanted silence and he played in silence.

Outside nothing could be heard but shots which seemed to be fired to keep the war going.

*   *   *

There was a roar of rifle-fire close by.

It continued. Roy put down his cards and went off to investigate.

"That's their Lordships enjoying themselves," he said to Guillaume as he took up his cards again. "Plouardec and Lulu are on duty at the listening post and they are playing manille. They took it into their heads to announce their points by firing shots. I've made them stop it."

The marines are not on the same terms as other soldiers with their commanding officers. They nickname the others 'fighters.' For example, they salute their commanders like infantry commanders replying to a private, accompanying the gesture with a friendly grin.

Twelve minutes after Roy's reprimand, the shots broke out again with renewed force.

Roy was furious. He smiled.

"This time they have gone too far. I shall punish

them. Come on, Guillaume," he said.

They were about to mount the platform in front of the listening posts, when they heard a voice, distant, but very clear and strong.

"Little beggars!" it snapped, in excellent French, "you're having a fine time keeping everyone awake. Wait till I tell your commanders!"

"Tell your commanders" meant order his men to fire.

"I ordered them to fire," yelled Roy.

The German voice, the fire, everything, relapsed into silence.

This much and no more is sanctioned by both sides.

This conversation will sound unlikely to anyone who is not familiar with the spirit of neighbourliness in a long war, and the family feeling of the marines.

*   *   *

The card game had been resumed. It seemed to be going on for ever when the telephone rang. Roy lifted the receiver. The line was bad. The wires had been laid in a hurry, and they crossed and touched each other. The noises of the sector filled the instrument like the ocean roaring in a shell.

"It's impossible to understand," he said. "I'm hanging up. I can only make out one thing, that is that it's Post F," (Post F was three miles away) "and they can't send a man to me. I haven't a man either. I don't like to risk a youngster's life for the sake of a message. These stupid men of mine have no sense of danger. They won't take their time, and they won't realize that you don't whistle, yap and stick your neck out thirty-five yards away from the Germans."

"That's easy," said Guillaume at that point. "I don't whistle and I don't yap. I even crawl, if necessary. I shall only have to take the long way round. I'll go."

Roy refused. Guillaume insisted. As Roy secretly wanted to be alone in his misery, as the long way round was not dangerous, and Guillaume was secretly overjoyed at this night excursion, they came to an agreement.

Guillaume would go and bring his message straight back to Roy.

The cold night was studded with white flares and stars. Guillaume found himself alone there for the first time. The last veil was lifted. Child and fairy became one. At last Guillaume knew what love was.

Instead of taking the long way round, he followed the parapet of the front line to the polder where he had to crawl. Breuil and he were expert at this Red Indian exercise.

A few yards further on, he came across a corpse. Someone had flung this body aside hastily. He studied it with a hard stare of curiosity.

He went on. He passed other corpses thrown aside in the massacre like the collar, boots, shirt and tie of a drunk undressing.

The mud made it difficult to go on all fours. Sometimes it makes the going smooth for the traveller and sometimes it tries to hold him back with the generous kiss of a nurse.

Guillaume stopped, waited and set off again. Here, he was alive in every fibre.

He was not thinking of Henriette nor of Madame de Bormes when he suddenly saw Madame de Bormes in his mind's eye.

He had just recognized the place in the trench,

disfigured by the mines, where she had complained
of feeling shaky a few days before.

We've been lucky all the same, he said to himself. We always think the sector is too quiet. The
princess was more astute than us. She might almost
have foreseen the fate of this trench.

A heap of knife-rests and barbed wire blocked
the way.

To go round to the left of it meant going up to
the thighs in water. Guillaume went to the right.

He came out on terra firma and was feeling
thankful for the total absence of revealing flares,
when he came to a sudden stop.

Some distance away in front of him he could
see the shape of an enemy patrol.

The patrol could see Guillaume and it did not
move. It thought it was invisible.

Guillaume's heart beat rhythmically, pounding
like a miner at the bottom of a mine.

The immobility became unbearable. He thought
he heard a challenge.

"Fontenoy!" he yelled at the top of his voice,
turning his fabrication into a war-cry. And as he
ran at a tremendous pace, he added, for fun,
"Guillaume II."

Guillaume raced, leapt, and rushed downhill like a hare.

As he heard no fire he stopped and turned round, out of breath.

Then he felt a stick strike him violently on the chest. He fell. He became deaf and blind.

A bullet. *I haven't a chance if I don't pretend to be dead*, he said to himself.

But in him make-believe and reality were one. Guillaume Thomas was dead.

*   *   *

The first person in Paris to be informed was Pesquel-Duport. At least, that was most likely. He was informed as the organizer of the canteens.

The good man could not believe it, for all the proofs.

He foresaw what a thunderbolt the news would be in the avenue Montaigne. He grieved over Madame de Bormes' grief.

What he did not admit, or only half admitted, was that although it was a dreadful solution, this death was a solution none the less. It put a full stop to the adventure, and meant that he could keep the secret of the Fontenoy story.

Poor Guillaume, he said to himself. The supposed uncle would not disown such a nephew. Killed in the North, he deserves the child Septentrion's epitaph: — danced for two days and found favour.

He had to tell his aunt and the women. The Editor would have liked to put off the second proceeding, but did not want the unfortunate women to hear of the disaster indirectly; he decided to go and see Guillaume's aunt, then on to the avenue Montaigne.

He was not reckoning on Madame Valiche.

While he did his sad duty in Montmartre, and Mademoiselle Thomas, after a moment's silence, gave a reply which amazed the unbeliever—"Thank you. I will see him soon. I will tell him about your visit," Madame Valiche was turning into the avenue Montaigne from the roundabout of the Champs-Elysées.

She was not reflecting on the trip to the lines, nor the compartment, nor how the convoy had been broken up by a whim of Guillaume's.

Her revenge was afoot.

This vampire knew of all the deaths from

Belgium to Alsace before anyone else. She had
heard of Guillaume's through one of Gentil's
brothers, a major at Zuydecôte, who had come
back on leave that morning.

He had put it in this form: — "a show-off, who
only got what he deserved." And so she was taking
it to Henriette and Madame de Bormes while it
was still warm.

The two women, who dared not go far away
from their flat for fear of missing Guillaume's reply
to Henriette's letter by one minute, were just going
out shopping.

They met Madame Valiche in the hall. Her
solemn manner alarmed them. They went back
into the drawing-room with her.

Madame Valiche knew how to strike home.

"I told you so," she said simply.

*   *   *

Henriette was the first to sense the disaster.

She pounced on Madame Valiche.

The wretched woman made short work of her
victims. When Pesquel-Duport entered the drawing-
room, he had missed the kill.

129

Madame de Bormes and her daughter were
screaming and tearing their dresses. Madame
Valiche stood in front of them making up details.

Pesquel-Duport grabbed her by the skirt.

"You! You!" he spluttered, "will you be so good
as to clear out right away."

He shook her and drew her towards the hall
door. He could have crushed her to death.

He threw her out.

What did it matter to Madame Valiche? She
put her hat straight, ran downstairs and rushed
home.

Gentil was at dinner, attacking the hors d'oeuvre.

"You can pat me on the back," she shouted from
the doorway. "I've seen what I wanted to see.
Mother and daughter. Two birds with one stone."

She hoped, at last, to dazzle this man who took
advantage of her and knew the value of simulating
imperturbability with cases of hysterics.

"Upper-class manners and nothing else," said he,
buttering a piece of bread.

Flushed with love and satisfied hatred, Madame
Valiche stared at this man who ate and lived his
life above surprise.

"Doctor, you are a god," she stammered.

"There are no gods, Madame. I can see through things, that's all."

*　　　　*　　　　*

The after-effects of the shock were too much for Mademoiselle de Bormes.

Madame de Bormes took her to a sanatorium at Auteuil. Two months later she died of a nervous disease which was not fatal. That is to say that in spite of the precautions, she poisoned herself.

Her mother became an old woman overnight. She only saw Pesquel-Duport.

"Let's get married. You can't live alone," he said.

"Wait," replied the princess. "Now you are too young. We're most unlucky with our ages. But they will match one day."

*　　　　*　　　　*

At Nieuport, near the church, the marines' cemetery is an unmoored brig.

A broken mast marks the centre.

131

Does the brig carry opium? A deep sleep enfolds the crew.

On every grave there is an attractive array of shells, pebbles, old fire-dogs, old door-frames, and old railings. One of them bears the name of Jacques Roy.

Jacques Roy died of a wound received at Saint-Georges, at the Nieuport dressing station in the space of four hours, glad to be avenging Pajot and Guillaume, for whose deaths he held himself responsible.

His cross bears the official inscription.

But on the next cross are the words: —

"G.—T. de Fontenoy. Gave his life for us."